CINCINNATUS
GEORGE WASHINGTON
AND THE ENLIGHTENMENT

BOOKS BY GARRY WILLS

CINCINNATUS
  GEORGE WASHINGTON AND THE ENLIGHTENMENT
LEAD TIME
THE KENNEDY IMPRISONMENT
EXPLAINING AMERICA
CHESTERTON
POLITICS AND CATHOLIC FREEDOM
ROMAN CULTURE
JACK RUBY
THE SECOND CIVIL WAR
NIXON AGONISTES
BARE RUINED CHOIRS
CONFESSIONS OF A CONSERVATIVE
INVENTING AMERICA
AT BUTTON'S

This book was first delivered as the W. W. Cook Lectures at the University of Michigan Law School. Parts of it were also given as the Doubleday Lecture at the Smithsonian Institution's National Museum of American History, as a Trumbull Memorial Lecture at the Yale Art Museum's one hundred and fiftieth anniversary, as the Massachusetts Historical Society's Boston Public Library Lecture, and as a paper at Temple University's seminar on the bicentennial of Washington's resignation. I am grateful to my hosts and the participants in all these events.

I am also grateful to those who read an earlier draft of the book and made helpful suggestions: Thomas Crow, Marcus Cunliffe, Ulysse Desportes, John Hallam, Edmund Morgan, David Van Zanten, and Robert Wiebe. Hunter Rawlings III helped me with his special knowledge of classical history. M. Elizabeth Scott, Curator of Slides at the Johns Hopkins History of Art Department, did indispensable service in acquiring the illustrations.

OVERLEAF:
FRONTISPIECE   Jean-Antoine Houdon,
Richmond statue of Washington

CINCINNATUS

GEORGE WASHINGTON
AND THE ENLIGHTENMENT

❮❮❮ ❮❮❮ ❮❮❮ ❮❮❮ ❮❮❮

GARRY WILLS

DOUBLEDAY & COMPANY, INC.
GARDEN CITY, NEW YORK
1984

DESIGN BY BEVERLEY VAWTER GALLEGOS

Library of Congress Cataloging in Publication Data
Wills, Garry, 1934–
Cincinnatus: George Washington and the Enlightenment.
Bibliography: p.
Includes index.
1. Washington, George, 1732–1799—Addresses, essays, lectures.
2. Enlightenment—Addresses, essays, lectures.
3. Heroes—United States—Addresses, essays, lectures.
4. United States—Intellectual life—1783–1865—Addresses,
essays, lectures. I. Title.
E312.62.W54 1984   973.4'1'0924   81–43152
ISBN 0-385-17562-0

to the memory of

JIM ANDREWS
editor and friend

CONTENTS

CONTENTS

LIST OF ILLUSTRATIONS

COLOR ILLUSTRATIONS

1   Grant Wood, *Parson Weems' Fable* (1939)
. . . deflation to pious fable

INTRODUCTION

Washington eludes us, even in the city named for him. Other leaders are accessible there—Lincoln brooding in square-toed rectitude at his Monument, a Brady image frozen in white, throned yet approachable; Jefferson democratically exposed in John Pope's aristocratic birdcage. Majestic, each; but graspable.

Washington's faceless Monument tapers off from us however we come at it—visible everywhere, and perfect; but impersonal, uncompelling. Yet we should remember that this Monument, unlike the other two, was launched by private efforts. When government energies were stalled, in the 1830s, subscriptions kept the project alive. Even when Congress took over the project, stones were added by the citizenry, those memorial blocks one can study while descending the long inner stairway. The classical control of the exterior hides a varied and spontaneous interior—an image of the puzzle that faces us, the early popularity of someone lifted so high above the populace. The man we can hardly find was the icon our ancestors turned to most easily and often. We are distanced from him by their generosity, their willingness to see in him something almost more than human.

Washington was the kind of man legends naturally grow up around. We can trace the way one such tale arose. In 1776, the new British Commander in Chief Lord Howe sent under flag of truce a letter to "George Washington, Esq." Washington consulted with his fellow officers and decided he must receive any missives under his official title, to guarantee the rights of war for his army. The

British kept trying to treat Americans as riotous British subjects, not an enemy in the field. A second letter came, addressed to "George Washington, Esq., &ca, &ca," and was also refused. What title would gain access? Washington's aides set the terms: "His Excellency, General Washington." An officer came from Howe using that form; but when he was admitted to the General's presence, after calling him "Excellency," he put the second letter on the table, with its "&ca, &ca" address. Washington refused to touch the letter, but took a verbal message from the man who asked for "General Washington" (Freeman 4.138–39, Flexner 2.102–3).

That episode was soon condensed and heightened to the form a French officer heard when he arrived at the American camp:

One of the company (if I remember rightly, it was, I think, Colonel Hamilton, who was afterwards so unfortunately and prematurely snatched from the hopes of his country) related the manner in which the General had received a dispatch from Sir Henry Clinton [sic], addressed to "Mr. Washington." Taking it from the hands of the flag of truce and seeing the direction, "This letter," said he, "is directed to a planter in the state of Virginia. I shall have it delivered to him, after the end of the war; till that time it shall not be opened." A second dispatch was addressed to His Excellency General Washington (Chinard 41).

The popular version of the incident has been tugged toward a regular folk motif, that of the shrewd underdog outwitting his superior. As Lawrence Levine has noticed, this is a recurring type in American slave tales (*Black Culture and Black Consciousness,* 121–38). In its new form, the story of Lord Howe's letter "says" that the British expected Washington to be simpleminded enough to fall into their trap, to accept dispatches as a private citizen. The second thing it "says" is that Washington slyly let the British know he was onto their game. The altered tale is an analytical gloss on what happened, one that brings out the meaning of the more complicated transaction it claims to report.

But it does more than that. It shows Americans as a whole

outwitting their "superiors." Washington already stood for an entire people, before some observers even suspected there *was* a people. Before there was a nation—before there was any symbol of that nation (a flag, a Constitution, a national seal)—there was Washington. Even when, in the course of revolutionary events, a flag did appear, and a Constitution, they did not have a long tradition behind them, to halo them with sacred memories. But Washington was still there, steadying the symbols, lending strength to them instead of drawing it from them.

New governments need symbols of stability; Machiavelli and Rousseau thought this was the reason so many states had been founded on divine oracles. Both read the legend of Theseus bringing the god's word from Delphi as an expression of political necessity. Even when Madison was proposing, in *The Federalist,* a new government, he asked that it be treated as an old one, given "that veneration, which time bestows on everything" (No. 49, Cooke 340). Washington's importance to the nation lay in his capacity for eliciting the veneration not yet given to less personal symbols of republican order. He was the embodiment of stability within a revolution, speaking for fixed things in a period of flux.

I shall be looking, in this book, at the way educated artists and propagandists shaped a deliberately didactic image of the nation's first great leader. But the populace had anticipated them. The learned Reverend Weems invented the cherry tree tale; but anonymous storytellers invented the tales of Washington throwing coins or other objects across the Rappahannock. Here, too, we can trace the literal basis for all later embroiderings. Washington was prodigiously strong, with long arms and huge hands that made him good at poling barges and throwing weights. The painter Charles Willson Peale observed this when he went to Mount Vernon before the Revolution to paint the first picture Washington ever sat for:

One afternoon, several young gentlemen, visitors at Mount Vernon, and myself engaged in pitching the bar, one of the athletic sports common in those times, when suddenly the Colonel appeared among us. He requested to be shown the pegs that marked the bounds of our effort; then, smiling, and without putting off his coat, held out his hand for the missile. No sooner did the heavy iron bar feel the grasp of his mighty hand than it lost the power of gravitation, and whizzed through the air, striking the ground far, very far, beyond our utmost limits. We were indeed amazed, as we stood around all stripped to the buff, with shirt sleeves rolled up, and having thought ourselves very clever fellows, while the Colonel, on retiring, pleasantly observed, "When you beat my pitch, young gentlemen, I'll try again" (Freeman 3.293).

Reports of Washington's strength—and of his quick reflexes, his horsemanship, his grace as a dancer—were true, and had a great deal to do with the magnifying of his feats. He *looked* a victor even in defeat. Peale's story already has the components of legend: the improbable late appearance of a champion, who, working under a severe handicap, does the apparently impossible—Robin Hood coming out of nowhere to beat the archer who had already put his arrow in the target's center. Washington, older than Peale and his fellow competitors, not stripped for action like them, without a chance to warm up, effortlessly sets a mark they have no hope of reaching.

In some stories told of him, the superhuman aspect of the man has endangered his humanity instead of enhancing it. This is especially true of tales still taken for truths, by scholars as well as the populace. Few readers are fooled, now, by the cherry tree; but another invention is regularly recounted as history—the story that Gouverneur Morris bet his friends at the Philadelphia convention he would have the nerve to pat the dignified Washington on the back in a familiar way. Washington met this gesture with a stare that froze Morris to the spot. The first record we have of this story appeared as thirdhand gossip in a book printed eighty years after the purported event—in Martin Van Buren's posthumous book on the political parties. From there it was repeated in James Parton's 1874 life of Jefferson, whence Max Farrand took it for inclusion in his record of the Philadelphia convention (3.85). From that source it has been endlessly parroted. This is a flimsy foundation for a story so entirely out of character for both men. Washington stoically endured familiarities from far less attractive acquaintances than Morris—from the boorish Gilbert Stuart and the clownishly manipulative Hugh Henry Brackenridge. Since that time, in his teens, when he copied out the rules of civility, Washington made it a point to defer to others whenever that was possible. And Morris was too urbane to overreach himself so obviously.

Where did this story come from? From two quite different sources—from some actual (and famous) words of Morris, and from a pattern in religious narratives. Morris's eulogy to Washington, the most famous and eloquent one after that of Henry Lee, included these words:

Heaven, in giving him the higher qualities of the soul, had given also the tumultuous passions which accompany greatness, and frequently tarnish its lustre. With them was his first contest, and his first victory was over himself. So great was the empire he had acquired there that calmness of manner and conduct distinguished him through life. Yet those who have seen him strongly moved will bear witness that his wrath was terrible. They have seen, boiling in his bosom, passion almost too mighty for man; yet when just bursting into act, that strong passion was controlled by his stronger mind. Having thus a perfect command of himself, he could rely on the full exertion of his powers, in whatever direction he might order them to act . . . Hence it was that he beheld not only the affairs that were passing around him, but those also in which he was personally engaged, with the coolness of an unconcerned spectator (*Eulogies* 44–45).

Even as they stand, these words suggest the main features of the later story—that Morris had witnessed an anger barely suppressed; that Washington, hot within, was cool without; that this made his very manner commanding. But one more sentence from the eulogy could serve as caption for the later tale: "None was great in his presence." Morris is saying that no one could measure up to Washington; but the line, when turned into anecdote, both trivializes and dangerously inflates Morris's message—trivializes it, since Washington is made too petulant to bear familiarities, and inflates it, because the result resembles tales that suggest the holy is *untouchable*. The scene is that often depicted in religious art, of Jesus in the garden warning the Magdalen off: *Noli me tangere.*

Where truth and rumor are so intimately interwoven, it may seem idle to seek the "real" Washington, especially since the legends were framed for tastes far different from ours. Generations of Americans grew up admiring the Washington of Parson Weems, who trivializes the man, in our eyes, by turning his life into a moral fable (Figure 1). Horatio Greenough, by contrast, deprives us of the human by rendering the god (Figure 2). Weems deflates, Greenough inflates; the result is the same. How can we approach Washington across the debris of so many broken idols?

Yet we should not, even if we could, simply sweep all that rubbish away, to arrive at the "real" man. More than most men, this man *was* what he meant to his contemporaries. If he played a necessary role at the birth of our republic, it is important for us to assess the expectations of his audience, along with his willingness consciously to meet those expectations. That means we must understand the Enlightenment's conception of political heroism. Once we do that, even Weems and Greenough will seem less trivializing than we thought. The way Washington conceived his task, and went about it, was tempered from the outset by the responses he hoped to elicit from his countrymen. His life verged on legend, even as he lived it, because he had models he was trying to live up to; and he came close enough for others to accept him as a literal fulfillment of the age's aspirations. This was nowhere more true than in the three great moments which seemed, for his contem-

2   Horatio Greenough, *George Washington*
. . . inflation to divine irrelevance

poraries, to sum up his life—the resignation of his commission as Commander in Chief, his sponsorship of the new Constitution in 1787, and his surrender of the presidency by a farewell address. It was in the performance of these acts that Washington became "larger than life," since each seemed to revive the ancient republic that men were yearning for. My book will consider each of those three acts, and the symbols through which early Americans tried to express their significance.

PART ONE

THE RESIGNATION

❮❮- ❮❮- ❮❮- ❮❮-

SECULAR CHARISMA

3   George Richardson, "Patriotism," from *Iconology* (1799)
. . . the surrender of trophies

I

FROM NEWBURGH
TO ANNAPOLIS

And when his fortune set before him all
The pomps and pleasures that his soul can wish,
His rigid virtue will accept of none.
—Addison, *Cato* 1.4

HE WAS A VIRTUOSO of resignations. He perfected the art of getting power by giving it away. He tried this first, unsuccessfully, as a young colonel of militia—but then only as a gesture from hurt pride. He was still learning that mere power to refuse is real, but limited. The power would later be refined, as would the gestures—when he learned the creative power of surrender.

Unlike other officers in the Revolution, he did not resign or threaten to resign when baffled of honor or advantage (GW 10.463). He did not want to cheapen the currency; he would not anticipate his promised abdication at war's end. His whole war service was urged forward under the archway of two pledges—to receive no pay, and to resign when independence was won. He was choreographing his departure with great care. It was an act of pedogogical theater; and the world applauded.

He tells us later what care he took to underline the meaning of his act. Pressed to rejoin the struggle for a stronger union in

3

1787, he wrote John Jay that he had escaped from that "sea of troubles":

Nor could it be expected, that my sentiments and opinion would have much weight on the minds of my Countrymen; they have been neglected, *tho' given as a last legacy in the most solemn manner* (GW 27.503, italics added).

He is referring to the circular letter sent to the governors of all thirteen states, during the summer of 1783, in which he announced his forthcoming resignation and coupled it with a plea for a more vigorous central government. He wanted the resignation at Annapolis to be seen as lending moral force to the arguments he had advanced to the governors.

He gave the matter careful thought, with an eye to timing as well as content. He would stage his lesson to men's eyes, not merely address their minds. The job he had given himself required great tact, an awareness of others' sensibilities, and an assurance that he was not overstepping his authority. The circular letter itself must be carefully phrased, and the situation of the Army had to be presented in just the right way. Washington had addressed circular letters to the governors during the war, but these were respectful pleas that the will of Congress be done in meeting particular crises. Besides, while the war was being actively waged, Washington had to be guarded in his language, since the posting of so many copies of a single letter made it probable that one or more would fall into enemy hands (GW 25.188). Now he meant to advance a proposal of his own, and one that fell more within the political than the military sphere.

He would not have undertaken this risky act were it not for his sense of the crisis that would follow on a victory; and he coupled the recommendation with his own pledge to resign not only his military commission but all future public office, lest the argument be read as a way of promoting his career. The resignation would give him moral standing for the circular letter. As he put it later to Governor Harrison of Virginia, a strengthened government would not directly profit him:

For my own part, altho' I am returned to, and am now mingled with the class of private citizens, and like them must suffer all the evils of a Tyranny, or of too great an extension of federal powers, I have no fears arising from this source (GW 27.306).

The same argument formed the basis of his appeal to the governors:

I will therefore speak to your Excellency, the language of freedom and of sincerity, without disguise; I am aware, however, that those who differ from me in political sentiment, may perhaps remark, I am stepping out of the proper line of my duty, and they may possibly ascribe to arrogance or ostentation, what I know is alone the result of the purest intention, but the rectitude of my own heart, which disdains such unworthy motives, the part I have hitherto acted in life, the determination I have formed, of not taking any share in public business hereafter, the ardent desire I feel, and shall continue to manifest, of quietly enjoying in private life, after all the toils of war, the benefits of a wise and liberal Government, will, I flatter myself, sooner or later convince my Countrymen, that I have no sinister views in delivering with so little reserve, the opinions contained in this Address (GW 26.486–87).

The other factor requiring delicacy on Washington's part was the situation of the Army. It was an excruciating task for Washington to maintain morale and discipline during the two years of "phony peace" that stretched from the battle at Yorktown to the departure of British troops from American soil. Washington could not relax so long as there was any possibility of a breakdown in the treaty negotiations—something that seemed quite possible after De Grasse, the victor at Yorktown, was himself defeated by Admiral Rodney off the island of Dominica, removing British fears for their hold on Jamaica. Washington was forced to treat all rumors of an early peace as tricks of the enemy, attempts to make the American Army disband before the British had departed (GW 25.267–68). But this, in turn, made it look as if he were clinging to power at the very moment when he was hoping to surrender it. Meanwhile, officers and men were looking toward their future, with a growing suspicion that Congress would not or could not honor the promises by which they had been recruited. Even where this discontent did not lead to actual or threatened mutiny, it threatened the public good will, the pride in the fighting forces, on which Washington hoped to base his plea for a union that would reflect the *continental* consciousness forged within his Army. As civilian-military tension mounted, Washington felt that the chance to use victory as the basis for a stable political order was slipping away from him. The wearisome time of neither peace nor war tried his patience as sorely as military setbacks ever had: "The predicament in which I stand, is as critical and delicate as can well be conceived" (GW 25.186).

After Yorktown, Washington had briefly hoped that he could, for the first time in the war, leave winter camp to visit Mount Vernon. But he soon realized that his presence was still called for. Complaints in the Army "will oblige me to stick very close to the Troops this Winter [1782] and to try like a careful physician to prevent if possible the disorders getting to an incurable height" (GW 25.270). Despite all his efforts, mutinous talk grew in the Army, fostered by Washington's old rival, Horatio Gates, who was with him at the winter camp in Newburgh. What made the matter doubly ticklish was the fact that some members of Congress, who desired the stronger union that Washington was sponsoring, thought they could advance their cause by playing on the Army's grievances, on the inability of the central government to address its complaints. Nothing could stand at a greater distance from Washington's moral argument for increased authority than any attempt to *seize* power, or to form it on a military basis.

Washington sent uncharacteristically stern warnings to Alexander Hamilton, letting him know that he realized what Hamilton and Robert Morris were up to. They must be brought to realize that "the Army (considering the irritible state it is in, its sufferings and composition) is a dangerous instrument to play with" (GW 26.293). Washington's political wisdom shows clearly in the urgency of these warnings (ibid. 208, 213). Since Washington would be obliged to oppose the schemers, he let them know in advance that their meddling "might create such divisions in the Army as would weaken, rather than strengthen the hands of those who were disposed to support Continental measures" (ibid. 324). Washington's work to establish the principle of civilian supremacy is usually based on the rebuke to the officers at Newburgh. At least as important were these earlier warnings sent to the schemers in Congress.

When that has been said, however, one must admire the tact with which he handled the discontented officers. Scheduling his own special meeting, preempting the anonymous call to consider revolt, he praised the Army for its standard of public service. Though he knew the role General Gates was playing, he let Gates assume the chair before his arrival, and pretended that the anonymous letter came from an "outside agitator," since it was so obviously below the honor of those assembled before him. Skillfully, Washington took the call to mutiny as a great *opportunity* for the men to display, in dramatic terms, their public virtue. (The assembly hall in which he spoke had been nicknamed by the Army "the Temple of Virtue"):

You will give one more distinguished proof of unexampled patriotism and patient virtue, rising superior to the pressure of the most complicated sufferings; and you will, by the dignity of your Conduct, afford occasion for Posterity to say, when speaking of the glorious example you have exhibited to Mankind, "had this day been wanting, the World had never seen the last stage of perfection to which human nature is capable of attaining" (ibid. 227).

Though Freeman argues that the rhetoric is Jonathan Trumbull's, the psychological tactics are characteristically Washingtonian, and the only draft we have of the address is the one he wrote in his own large hand, so he would have no trouble reading it. Washington's intimate participation in the composition of the address is indicated by a reference to one of his favorite lines from his favorite play, Addison's *Cato:* "In the mild lights of calm philosophy" (ibid. 226).

Only when Washington tried to read an excerpt from a congressional dispatch did the most famous moment occur, that touch of theater with which he drew out his new pair of glasses and adjusted them to read. The necessity for the glasses was unfeigned; he had recently thanked David Rittenhouse, the mechanical genius of Philadelphia, for grinding their lenses:

The Spectacles suit my Eyes extremely well, as I am persuaded the reading glasses also will when I get more accustomed to the use of them. At present I find some difficulty in coming at the proper Focus; but when I do obtain it, they magnify properly and show objects very distinctly which at first appear like a mist blended together and confused (ibid. 137).

It is not his use of the glasses that reduced some in his audience to tears, but the words he spoke while getting the congressional document at the right distance to focus on its contents: "Gentlemen, you must pardon me. I have grown grey in your service and now find myself growing blind" (Freeman 5.435).

Actually, the crowning touch of theater was given when Washington folded up the letter and left the hall, signaling by his manner that it was unthinkable anyone would defend the anonymous call to mutiny—despite the fact that Gates still sat in the chair as the highest-ranking officer after Washington. He had gauged his men well. Though Timothy Pickering tried to turn the gathering's mind back to the anonymous address, he was silenced by a motion of thanks for General Washington's intervention. The impact of Washington's appearance was registered by one of those present, Samuel Shaw:

On other occasions, he had been supported by the exertions of an Army and the countenance of his friends; but in this he stood single and alone. There was no saying where the passions of an Army, which were not a little inflamed, might lead; but it was generally allowed that longer forebearance was dangerous, and moderation had ceased to be a virtue. Under these circumstances he appeared, not at the head of his troops, but as it were in opposition to them; and for a dreadful moment the interests of the Army and its General seemed to be in competition. He spoke— every doubt was dispelled, and the tide of patriotism rolled again in its wonted course (ibid. 436).

Washington, as usual, gave the credit for this outcome to his men. He had a gift for shaming them into actions above themselves, and then praising what he had made them become. In forwarding to Congress the respectful petition drawn up in consequence of the meeting he had called, Washington wrote:

The result of the proceedings of the grand Convention of the Officers, which I have the honor of enclosing to your Excellency for the inspection of Congress, will, I flatter myself, be considered as the last glorious proof of patriotism which could have been given by Men who aspired to the distinction of a patriot Army; and will not only confirm their claim to the justice, but will increase their title to the gratitude of their Country (GW 26.229).

There is no mention of his own address at the meeting. He would erase, if he could, all memory of division between himself and other officers; he goes on, in this letter, to advocate the officers' cause as ardently as any of the mutineers could have wished. The ranks were reunited.

But not everywhere. When a Pennsylvania garrison broke out in mutiny, Washington sent picked troops to break their revolt and, at the same time, wrote Congress to defend the Army's honor:

I feel an expressible satisfaction, that even this behaviour cannot stain the name of the American Soldiery; it cannot be imputable to, or reflect dishonour on the army at large; but on the contrary, it will, by the striking contrast it exhibits, hold up to public view the other Troops, in the most advantageous point of light . . . for when we consider that these Pennsylvania Levies who have now mutinyed, are Recruits and Soldiers of a day, who have not borne the heat and burden of the War, and who can have in reality very few hardships to complain of, and when we at the same time recollect, that those Soldiers who have lately been furloughed from this Army, are the Veterans who have patiently endured hunger, nakedness and cold, who have suffered and bled without a murmur, and who with perfect good order have retired to their homes, without the settlement of their Accounts or a farthing of money in their pockets, we shall be as much astonished at the virtues of the latter, as we are struck with horror and detestation at the proceedings of the former (GW 27.33).

Having kept the Army (for the most part) virtuous in the eighteenth-century sense—i.e., public-spirited—he must now defend that virtue. Only then, appealing to the national gratitude, could he make his plea for a closer expression of national spirit within the government itself.

The timing of the plea was important. It should not be issued till victory was assured and the tasks of waging war had been eased. But if Washington waited till the signing of the definitive treaty (which came in September of 1783), or the departure of the British (which came in November), or his own actual resignation (on December 23), his message might be overlooked in the hubbub of celebration and emotional relief. So, after careful drafting, he sent out his circular letter early in June, when word of the treaty was anxiously awaited but debate about its terms could not begin. For Washington, his "Legacy" (as the letter was soon being called) and his resignation were two aspects of a single process, moving from the events at Newburgh through the dispatching of the letter, culminating in the resignation, at Annapolis, in December. It had been a tortuous course to steer, and he saw his project threatened all along; yet he maneuvered his way at last to the fullfillment of his pledge.

After the signing of the definitive treaty, in September, the British made their preparations to depart; but logistical difficulties lengthened yet again the wait for those Americans who longed to reenter New York in triumph. On November 20, Washington moved down from West Point to watch events at the Harlem River. The British had promised to depart on the twenty-third; but that day passed, and another, before a certain time was fixed for the city's evacuation—noon on the twenty-fifth. Washington was careful to let the civilian authorities reclaim their town; he rode in by the side of Governor Clinton, followed by New York's militia, not the continental troops (some of whom had taken shortcuts to be along the line of parade, cheering their leader). Washington's life had already become a series of farewells—to his troops, to their officers, to state legislatures, to the institutions past which he rode on his way to Annapolis (Princeton, the American Philosophical Society), to city councils, to numberless well-wishers. Each received a formal address of thanks, usually repeating Washington's pledge to leave public life forever. In his Final Orders to the troops, he addressed them as "one patriotic band of Brothers" (GW 27.224). Addressing others, he called them "my virtuous fellow Citizens in the field" (ibid. 239).

He reached Annapolis on the night of the nineteenth and asked Thomas Mifflin, the president of Congress, how he should submit his resignation:

I take the earliest opportunity to inform Congress of my arrival in this City, with the intention of asking leave to resign the Commission I have the honor of holding in their Service. It is essential for me to know their pleasure, and in what manner it will be most proper to offer my resignation, whether in writing, or at an Audience; I shall therefore request to be honored with the necessary information, that being apprized of the

4   John James Barralet, *General Washington's Resignation* (1799)
. . . the plow awaits the plowman

FROM NEWBURGH TO ANNAPOLIS

sentiments of Congress I may regulate my Conduct accordingly (ibid. 277–78).

A session was arranged for the morning of December 23, with a formal document of thanks to Washington drafted by Jefferson and others. When the General went into the statehouse, his horse was waiting at the door, to carry him to Mount Vernon by Christmas Eve. It was the last in a series of emotional partings, and his hand shook as he spoke what he took to be his last words on the public stage:

Having now finished the work assigned me, I retire from the great theater of Action; and bidding an Affectionate farewell to this August body under whose orders I have so long acted, I here offer my Commission, and take my leave of all the employments of public life (ibid. 285).

At that moment the ancient legend of Cincinnatus—the Roman called from his plow to rescue Rome, and returning to his plow when danger had passed—was resurrected as a fact of modern political life. The fame of the deed sped around the world. The painter John Trumbull wrote his brother from London (May 10, 1784) that it

excites the astonishment and admiration of this part of the world. 'Tis a Conduct so novel, so inconceivable to People, who, far from giving up powers they possess, are willing to convulse the Empire to acquire more.

Benjamin West, Trumbull's instructor, liked to tell the story of his conversation with King George III during the war. Asked what General Washington would do if he prevailed, West said he thought he would return to his farm. "If he does that," the King is supposed to have remarked, "he will be the greatest man in the world."

Trumbull and Charles Willson Peale both did early paintings, now lost, of Washington as Cincinnatus. The two greatest statues of the man—by Houdon, by Canova—would present him in the same role. And when Trumbull did his four large paintings for the Capitol rotunda, in Washington, the resignation was paired with the Declaration of Independence to show the range of civil heroism that went into the country's formation.

Trumbull gave Washington the pose of Patriotism from the emblem books—e.g., from Richardson's *Iconology* (Figure 3)—where the trophies of war are sacrificed to peace. John J. Barralet had used the same pose in his 1799 engraving *General Washington's Resignation* (Figure 4); but Barralet's Washington does not have his hand on his hip—he gestures away from the allegorical scene to a realistic team of oxen, hitched to their plow, in front of an accurate depiction of Mount Vernon. The scene of private felicity in the background is seen as the cause of public prosperity in the foreground, the cornucopia guarded by the eagle.

Trumbull, too, has placed private felicity on the right (the female) side of the picture, where he takes the liberty of introducing Martha into the gallery (Figure 5). Washington stands central to the picture, but lower than Thomas Mifflin, who—under the high pediment to the left—stands for the civil authority. The left side of the picture is entirely male, official, and political. Trumbull took the liberty of inserting Madison into the Congress of that period, so that the four Virginia presidents would all be present in it, suggesting the fertility of Washington's act, the progeny it would sire. The right side of the picture is, by comparison, relaxed, familiar, a conversation piece of relatives and friends. Washington has flung his riding cloak—already part of this scene's established iconography—to one side, suggesting the rapidity of his ride to Annapolis and his entry into the hall, the *unhesitating* surrender of power at the earliest possible moment. Only one touch of solemnity is added to this "domestic" side of the painting—the two grave men wrapped in robelike cloak and coat. They are "quoted" from the grieving parliamentarians in Copley's famous

5   John Trumbull, *The Resignation of General Washington* (1824–28)
   . . . the pivot of the republic

Death of Lord Chatham. Washington meant, of course, to make of his "Legacy" a kind of "deathbed statement" so far as any further political life was concerned. The force of his act is to be registered on the two men as they watch him turn and go out under the lower pediment on the right toward the peace and obscurity of his home.

    Though Trumbull had sketched the chamber in Annapolis, he removed the windows from the wall behind Washington and broadened the pilaster behind him, which suggests the stability of the republic. As in his companion picture of civil heroism, a light from no explicable source is thrown upon the symbolic background, the light of virtue derived from the act itself, making the architectural support of the whole fabric glow. Though the aging Trumbull had lost most of his skills by the time he did this painting (1824–28), it serves as a summary of the themes associated with Washington's resignation as people had the opportunity to meditate upon that act in the early days of the republic.

II

DICTATOR

Happy the people, who preserve their honour,
By the same duties, that oblige their Prince.
—Addison, *Cato* 2.5

GANDHI OPPOSED the translation of *satyagraha* as "passive resistance." He rightly considered his strategy a very *active* kind of advocacy, however nonviolent. In the same way, Washington's resignation was not a mere walking away from power. He had to use power most adroitly in order to give it up in useful ways. He had to steer through all the dangers of the half war into an even more dangerous time of half mutiny, which could have turned military victory into moral defeat. He had to prevail at Newburgh in order to resign at Annapolis. And he had to resign at Annapolis in order to deliver his Legacy. His whole war had been a matter of campaigning within the context of resigning. This double activity was increased as his strictly military duties dwindled. The resignation became a growing ideal throughout the final years of service, against which other things must be measured. All the impending dangers were endangering it. Opportunities must be seized to forward it. Letters of congratulation, exhortation, and farewell took their emotional tone from it. By the time the moment arrived, it both surprised people and struck them as inevitable. Washington

17

had staked his entire career and future influence on one *gran rifiuto,* not the kind Dante condemned in Celestine V, but the kind the Enlightenment was prepared to honor in a modern Cincinnatus.

In the short run, it is true, Washington's actions did not have their desired effect. Admiration for the teacher did not extend to an acceptance of his teaching. The closer union he had argued for did not come about in the first four years of peace: and even in 1787 the effort to pass the Constitution would probably have failed if Washington had not broken the pledge which he considered his best contribution to the republic. Some of Washington's warmest modern admirers are critical of him, not for breaking that pledge, but for being so loath, so slow, so reluctant to break it. They underestimate Washington's heavy emotional investment in the symbol of his resignation. He resisted the abandonment of that promise for the same reason he had resisted earlier attempts to involve him in state or federal office, and from the same instinct that made him seek, as soon as he had presidential power, the earliest opportunity for divesting himself of it.

His instinct in this matter was profoundly right. Everything else he was able to achieve rested on the confidence he had inspired by his resignation. Even when forced to break his pledge, he did so with such visible yielding to multiple demands on him that no one felt he had dishonored his word. The resignation was the thing most often praised in the eulogies at his death—more, even, than the forming of a new government, more than his surrendering of presidential power. These later things were correctly read as implied in the first great act.

There is another and deeper criticism of Washington, that he was afraid to use power as actively as he could have, to take greater risks for greater results, out of excessive regard for his personal equanimity and fame. It is a sin, in some political scientists' eyes, not to love power, to be happy in its exercise. These analysts are descendants of Thomas Carlyle, whose hero worship did not extend to the cautious and self-contained Washington: "A simple Diocletian prefers planting of cabbages; a George Washington, no very immeasurable man, does the like." Carlyle bridles at any subjection of Cromwell to "contrasts with Washington and others—above all, with those noble Pyms and Hampdens." Placid martyrs were not in Carlyle's line, any more than were calm winners of the Washington sort. He wants his men to knock their heads on stars or shoot beyond "this world's walls of fire" (*extra flammantia moenia mundi*).

Carlyle praises Cromwell because he refused to resign, because he believed that there was "nothing between England and utter Anarchy but him alone," so that "this Prime Minister could retire no-whither except into his tomb." But Carlyle gives the truth away when he admits that Cromwell "could not *get* resigned." That is the normal fate of charismatic leaders, who supplant institutional authority with their personal "grace," the only social glue remaining when all other bonds of cohesion have been loosed. Washington was charismatic in Max Weber's sense—he became the moving emblem of legitimacy in unsettled times. Yet he somehow avoided the fate of other charismatic leaders, who could neither pass on their authority nor relinquish it. Modern revolutions offer us the paradox that social changes most inspired by a vision of impersonal historical process have clung most devoutly to the image of a single leader—Stalin's, for decades, or Mao's. Even when there is a blurred *succession* of charismatic leaders—Lafayette, Mirabeau, Marat, Danton, Robespierre, etc.—they seem, so long as revolutionary spasms continue, to be endable only in one outsize icon: Napoleon. Magic flits from one man to another, or is held by one man in defiance of the reason for his original elevation. Reinhard Bendix notes the persistence of this problem in modern revolutions, those led by Nkrumah, Sihanouk, Kim, and others:

The new nations provide a setting of rapid change in which charismatic leaders may achieve new forms of political integration. In his analysis of *Ghana in Transition,* David Apter has suggested that charismatic leadership helps to make way for the creation of secular legal institutions in a nation-state. He notes, however, that charismatic leadership is not easily reconciled with secular systems of authority. Perhaps a charismatic leader like Nkrumah can transfer some of the loyalty traditionally accorded to tribal chiefs to his agents and symbols of a secular government—as long as he is the leader. But the problem is: How can the loyalties of a personal following be transferred to the institutions of government? (In *Max Weber,* ed. Dennis Wrong, 1970)

Charismatic leadership seems to offer insoluble problems of legitimate succession. To the extent that it is personal, it cannot be passed on. To the extent that it is at odds with institutional rule, it disrupts other forms of authority by establishing its own. How did Washington escape these traps?

He was helped by the ideology of classical republicanism which he came, in time, to embody. That ideology retained a vision of emergency powers given to some worthy man, who proves his worthiness by refusing to exercise the powers beyond that emergency's demands. Some of the Romans most admired in the eighteenth century had been *dictatores*—including the two Washington was most often compared with, Cincinnatus and Fabius. The office of *dictator,* like the *fasces,* had not yet acquired an evil modern resonance. In fact, Machiavelli and Rousseau praised the office for its *containment* of power. Where other nations give emergency powers to the government itself, stretching the letter of the law or breaking down its barriers, the Romans' declaration of a limitable time of peril kept response to it a matter of legal *extra*-legality.

Our own government has in modern times assumed powers hard to lay aside when danger (or apparent danger) faded—in times of war, for instance, or of rumored subversion. From the

Alien and Sedition Acts to the McCarthy period, civil rights were suspended in fact without open admission that the Constitution had been done any violence. The classical ideal was to describe the peril as narrowly as possible and commission a trustworthy man to cope with it over a defined period. The test of his trust was an unwillingness to extend the period of his power. As Rousseau put it:

Public morality made idle the precautions which would have been necessary at another time; there was no fear that a dictator would abuse his authority or try to extend it beyond the fixed time. Instead, so great a power seemed onerous to those who bore it, such was their haste to put it off, their feeling that it was troublesome and dangerous to supplant the laws (*Contrat* 4.6, Garnier ed. 324).

Machiavelli, in his *Discourses,* had praised dictatorship in the same terms: "Three things, then, worked together: the dictatorship lasted but a short time; the dictator's power was limited; the Roman people was not corrupt. These conditions made it impossible for the dictator to go beyond bounds" (Gilbert 1.268).

This concept of extraordinary powers, ceded on a temporary basis, lies behind the service of Washington in the war. When he went North to take charge of the continental Army, the New York legislature emphasized the moral contract implicit in his commission:

On a general in America, fortune also should bestow her gifts, that he may rather communicate lustre to his dignities than receive it, and that his country in his property, his kindred, and connexions, may have sure pledges that he will faithfully perform the duties of his high office, and readily lay down his power when the general weal requires it (GW 3.305).

Washington was quick to respond to this opportunity for honor. Speaking for his "worthy Colleagues" as well as himself, he wrote the New York legislature:

When we assumed the Soldier, we did not lay aside the Citizen; and we shall most sincerely rejoice with you in that happy hour when the establishment of American Liberty, upon the most firm and solid foundations, shall enable us to return to our Private Stations in the bosom of a free, peaceful and happy Country (ibid.).

The agreement to serve without recompense was a kind of hostage given to the ideal of Cincinnatus, a pledge that no *other* emolument would be sought. Congress praised him for taking power on these terms as, over the years, it grew more confident of his discretionary authority: "Happy it is for this country that the General of their forces can be entrusted with the most unlimited power, and neither personal security, liberty or property be in the least endangered thereby" (Freeman 4.338). Washington not only recognized the terms of service but underlined them in his response:

Instead of thinking myself freed from all *civil* obligations by this mark of confidence, I shall constantly bear in mind that as the sword was the last resort for the preservation of our liberties, so it ought to be the first to be laid aside when those liberties are firmly established (GW 6.464).

When, true to his trust, Washington returned his powers to their source, Congress applauded the virtue it had demanded in the original grant:

Called upon by your country to defend its invaded rights, you accepted the sacred charge, before it had formed alliances, and whilst it was without funds or a government to support you. You have conducted the great military contest with wisdom and fortitude, invariably regarding the rights of the civil power, through all disasters and changes . . . Having defended the standard of liberty in this new world: having taught a lesson useful to those who inflict, and to those who feel oppression, you retire from the great theatre of action, with the blessings of your fellow citizens; but the glory of your virtues will not terminate with your military command; it will continue to animate remotest ages (Marshall 4.624–25).

The Chevalier de Chastellux had already put the matter more succinctly: "This is the seventh year that he has commanded the army and that he has obeyed the Congress; more need not be said" (*Travels in America,* London, 1787, 1.137).

Unlike Carlyleans, who praise a happy thirst for power, men of the Enlightenment tried to instill a considered reluctance to exercise it. This was a standard Washington internalized, connecting it with his own equanimity and freedom from guilt. He acquired in the process a kind of moral gyroscope that kept him ungiddied by power. This attitude is revealed in his response to the semideification he received in the parade of triumph taking him North to the presidency. He wrote, on the night of his arrival in Manhattan:

The display of boats which attended and joined us on this occasion, some with vocal and some with instrumental music on board; the decorations of the ships, the roar of the cannon, and the loud acclamations of the people which rent the skies, as I passed along the wharves, filled my mind with sensations as painful (considering the reverse of this scene, which may be the case after all my labors to do good), as they are pleasing (*Diaries* 5.447).

Thus Washington's charisma came from a prominently displayed eagerness to transcend itself; he gained power from his readiness to give it up. And in accepting the ideal of Cincinnatus, Washington automatically limited the dangers of charismatic leadership, which is always at least quasi-religious, an assertion of semidivine "grace." Cincinnatus was an icon meant by the Enlightenment to *replace* churchly saints with a resolutely secular ideal. Here, too, Washington was fully in accord with the moral demands made on him. By inclination and principle, he shied from demonstrations of piety. Even Parson Weems had to supply a fictitious scene of prayer, because there was so little real display to dwell on. This was, in fact, so marked a deficiency in the eyes of the godly that Timothy Dwight felt a need to excuse his hero's lack of religious enthusiasm (*Discourses* 27–28).

It is true that Washington referred to the political importance of religion in his Farewell Address; but this utilitarian recommendation was enough, in itself, to separate him from the piety of his critics. He lists religion with education and public credit as so many props of "public felicity." Nor was this just a matter of accepting his ghostwriter's words. Flexner (4.300) shows how Washington softened Hamilton's original language on the importance of religion. When, in messages less thoroughly worked over by Washington himself, religious expressions crop up, they sometimes reflect the ardor of his New England ghostwriters. During the war, two "Connecticut Wits" in arms—Jonathan Trumbull and David Humphreys—made their commander speak with a religiosity that did not come naturally to the Virginian (Freeman 5.493).

Washington's presidential invocations of Providence do not outrun anything that Jefferson would be comfortable with when he reached the White House. And the first President's churchgoing was as dutiful as the third President's. As soon as he retired from his second term, Washington gave up the vestryman's duties expected of a man in his position, and manifested what Freeman called an "unwillingness to attend church" (6.3). His attitude emerges from this incident: "After the minister, annoyed that when Martha took communion the President waited in his pew, preached a sermon in Washington's presence concerning the duty of great men to set a good example, Washington never attended church again" (Flexner 4.490).

America's great leaders in the separation of church and state were the Virginians Madison and Jefferson. It is not often remarked that Washington shared their attitude. In fact, he exerted himself to prevent the formation of an official religion as early as 1777, when he opposed a congressional plan to appoint chaplains at the brigade level, overriding the local-preference pattern that had grown up informally in the appointment of chaplains. Washington wrote to John Hancock, the president of Congress:

I shall take occasion to mention, that I communicated the Resolution, appointing a Brigade Chaplain in the place of all others, to the several Brigadiers; they are all of the opinion, that it will be impossible for them to discharge the duty; that many inconveniences and much dissatisfaction will be the result, and that no Establishment appears so good in this instance as the Old One. Among many other weighty objections to the Measure, it has been suggested, that it has a tendency to introduce religious disputes into the Army, which above all things should be avoided, and in many instances would compel men to a mode of Worship which they do not profess. The old Establishment gives every regiment an Opportunity of having a Chaplain of their own religious Sentiments, it is founded on a more generous toleration . . . (GW 8.203–4).

Virginians in general supported religious tolerance and the secular state—partly, no doubt, because of the poor quality of clergymen sent to Virginia by the Anglican Church. It was Edmund Randolph who blocked Franklin's proposal to bring in a clergyman for prayer during one of the crises of the convention that drafted the 1787 Constitution. As Commander in Chief, Washington outlawed that favorite New England festivity "Pope's Day," since its "guying" of Fawkes-like victims was offensive to his Catholic soldiers. It was important to the success of the world's first truly secular state that its principal hero was glorified in Roman, not Christian, terms. This involved a deliberate abandoning of the first image that defined Washington's greatness, the image of Moses; and this secularizing of the man's role is best seen, ironically, in the work of the man who is always called *Parson* Weems.

6   John James Barralet, *Apotheosis of Washington* (1800)
. . . crossing of time and eternity

III

WEEMS AND CINCINNATUS

Be Cato's friend, he'll train thee up to great
And virtuous deeds.
                                    —Addison, *Cato* 2.4

AMERICA WAS a new thing, men hoped or feared, from the outset. But new in what way? As a new Israel, a Chosen People in the
wilderness? That was one of the first and most obvious ways of
looking at our novelty; and it has not entirely disappeared to this
day. Meaning tended to come, in colonial America, from the pulpit or the pamphlet, indiscriminately—there were journalists in
the pulpit and pastors in the coffeehouses. Their theme was inevitable. John Adams heard it in a Philadelphia sermon of May 17, 1776:

I have this morning heard Mr. Duffil upon the signs of the times. He
runs a parallel between the case of Israel and that of America, and between the conduct of Pharaoh and that of George.

Adams liked the symmetry of it, and had a delightful suspicion he
might be the deliverer in this new tale of exodus. He says in the
same letter, "Is it not a saying of Moses, who am I that I should
go out before this great people?"

But, poor John, who *was* he, finally, to play Moses in this
epic of American deliverance? Others had a more obvious candidate in mind. Earlier in that same year (March 17), a Cambridge

27

preacher chose his text from the book of Exodus (14.25): "And took off their chariot wheels that they drove them heavily, so that the Egyptians said, Let us flee from the face of Israel, for the Lord fighteth for them against the Egyptians" (Freeman 4.53). The city felt at once the force of that passage, since the British had just been driven from its streets, and its deliverer had come down from Dorchester Heights as from Mount Sinai. When the Rev. Abiel Leonard spoke of Moses, some eyes in the congregation were fixed on the tall Virginian attending their service that Sunday.

In time, very few heroes of ancient Israel would escape comparison with George Washington. For some writers, it was natural to compare him with later heroes of the Bible, since they had cast Christopher Columbus in the role of Moses. That still left an opportunity for Washington to play David, or Elijah, or Noah, or Joshua, or Hezekiah, or Josiah. The ingenious David Austin, who systematically drove himself mad in the 1790s by studying bible texts, saw Washington as the new Zerubbabel returning God's people from exile.

The most ambitious biblical treatment of Washington was Timothy Dwight's *Conquest of Canaan* (1785), which shows, in acute form, the problem Americans had in forging an identity for themselves. The battles are classical, the story biblical, as in Milton's epic; but Dwight must be "modern" as well, rhyming his couplets like Dryden or Pope. Odd bits of learning twist classical and sacred history toward some *tertium quid* that wants to call itself America. As Leon Howard put it: "Dwight's poem was full of eighteenth century Americans with Hebrew names who talked like Milton's angels and fought like prehistoric Greeks." And through it all stalks Washington, thinly disguised as Joshua:

> His form, majestic, seem'd by God designed
> The glorious mansion of so vast a mind.
> An awful grandeur in his countenance sate,
> Calm wisdom round him cast a solemn state (6.154).

Dwight not only adapts to Washington some verses from Dryden's *Don Sebastian;* he lights on the very ones Abigail Adams applied to Washington the first time she met him. Joshua is a hero of great self-restraint; but his one outburst of biblical wrath (against Ardan in Book 3) corresponds to Washington's legendary anger at the battle of Monmouth.

When Joshua's captains fall in battle, they are compared to American heroes. The death of Aram is like that of Dwight's acquaintance from Yale days, Nathan Hale:

> Thus, while fond Virtue wish'd in vain to save,
> Hale, bright and generous, found a hapless grave.
> With genius' living flame his bosom glow'd,
> And science charm'd him to her sweet abode.
> In worth's fair path his feet adventur'd far,
> The pride of peace, the rising grace of war.
> In duty firm, in danger calm as even,
> To friends unchanging, and sincere to heaven.
> How short his course, the prize how early won,
> While weeping friendship mourns her favorite gone (1.75–84).

When Uzal dies, in Book 8, he not only talks like Hale ("My nation own'd my life, and now demands my death") but is compared to another of the Revolution's fallen sons:

> Thus, hung with wounds, a prey to savage steel,
> In Princeton's fields the gallant Mercer fell (8.453–54).

George F. Sensabaugh has traced the ways Dwight tried to rival Milton. He succeeded in one way only—his heroes are so unremittingly noble, his heroines so refrigerant with virtue, that his villain, Hanniel, steals the show. Later Dwight would claim that Joshua was not intended for Washington; but Kenneth Silverman has shown he was trying to rewrite his own history to avoid rewriting his poem. The best proof that his Joshua is Washington comes from evidence that Hanniel is General Charles Lee, who had been cast as the villain at Monmouth. Dwight's 1800 *Discourse* on Washington describes Lee as the envious rival of Washington's greatness, "a foreigner in every respect his inferior" (18). In both the poem and the *Discourse,* Lee is given an evil prominence. In both, Washington prevails by a noble restraint, giving the schemer enough rope to hang himself: "Of this glaring attempt against him, his mind—superior alike to favor and to frown—took no other notice than what has been buried in silence" (19).

The 1800 *Discourse* shows that Dwight did not lose his admiration for Washington—if anything, his hardening federalism increased it. He tried to "take back" the Joshua comparison because, as the war receded from concern, he hoped his epic would live as pure art, not tied to passing events. Actually the reverse of that has happened. Most of the interest the poem retains is for its mythic picture of contemporary politics. If Thomas Otway's play, *Venice Preserved,* had no worth in itself, it would still be read as evidence of popular response to the Gunpowder Plot. *The Conquest of Canaan* comes to life only when Dwight sees the actual war around him through strange, biblical filters. We see what the British poet William Cowper could not in his 1788 review of the poem—that its Revolutionary references go far beyond the mention of specific martyrs:

A little mature consideration would have taught him [Dwight] that a subject nearly four thousand years old could not afford him a very fair opportunity for the celebration of his contemporaries. We found our attention to the wars of Joshua not pleasantly interrupted by a tribute of respect paid to the memory of a Mr. Wooster, slain on Ridgefield Hills in America; of a Mr. Warren, who fell in battle at Charlestown; and of a Mr. Mercer, who shared a similar fate at Princeton.

We take as cue what Cowper frowned on as intrusion. The stirrings of the "Conway Cabal" lie behind Book 3, the death of Revolutionary heroes behind Book 8, the humiliation of Charles

Lee at Monmouth behind Book 6. General Charles Lee (no relative of the Virginians) was a mysteriously charming blowhard, who shocked the ladies but somehow made men think his bluster could not *all* be based on lies. As Hamilton wrote in 1778, "A certain preconceived and preposterous opinion of his being a very great man will operate in his favor" (Freeman 5.57). Lee criticized with praise and undercut with flattery, wanting to fight when that was impossible, wanting to run when that was forbidden, theatrically loitering near wars as if he ran them. Unlike Washington, he *sought* the dictator's role: "I could do you much good, could I but dictate for one week" (Freeman 4.264). Dwight gives Hanniel Charles Lee's gifts:

> With friendly grasp he squeez'd each warrior's hand,
> With jests familiar pleas'd the vulgar band.
> In sly shrewd hints the Leader's faults disclos'd,
> Prais'd his whole sway, but single acts oppos'd.
> Admir'd how law so stern a face could wear;
> Styl'd combat rashness and nam'd caution fear.
> With angels then his fame and virtue join'd
> To tempt coarse scandal from each envious mind—
> Blest his own peaceful lot and smil'd that Heaven
> To "minds that priz'd them" empire's toils had given
>   (1.148–57).

In Hanniel's comparatively exciting presence, Dwight will even attempt wit: when Washington's Joshua rebukes the conspirators,

> Each saw, abash'd, the terrors of his frown
> And, pleas'd, condemn'd rebellion *not his own* (6.253–54).

There was something Luciferian in Lee that fascinated Connecticut's puritan Dwight. Already Washington is thrown in the shade by his own virtue, which is less colorful than Charles Lee's vice.

Despite continued Bible-rummaging for fresh comparisons, most men were forced back on Moses, if they did not begin with him, as Washington's obvious model. Dwight devoted his elaborately wrought 1800 eulogy to Washington's Mosaic traits. "Comparison with him," he admits, "is become almost proverbial" (17). But he says it is as appropriate as it is hackneyed: "The pre-eminence of Moses to all the great men of Israel, and the like distinction justly claimed by the American leader—not only over his countrymen but over all men of the present age—form a most honorable ground of comparison" (17). It was a theme that filled the oratory of Fourth of July celebrations. Elias Boudinot's 1793 speech called Washington "our miraculous deliverer from a second Egypt—another house of bondage." Five years later, the Reverend Cyprian Strong said: "In the case of the Hebrews God glorified and raised up Moses as the leader of the people. In like manner God raised up Washington" (ibid. 193). The 1800 funeral orations were filled with Mosaic texts and tributes. Josiah Dunham wrote: "It was Washington who confirmed to us the possession of this American Canaan; who, through a wilderness of dangers and a Red Sea of blood, stood (under God) our sheltering cloud by day and our pillar of fire by night."

Since, as Dwight said, reference to Moses was canonical by 1800, men exerted themselves in finding new facets to this comparison. In 1796 Richard Snowden compared the mist that allowed Washington's troops to slip away from Manhattan with the cloud of Moses (*Columbiad,* Canto 6):

> Just so looked Moses on the Egyptian coast
> Fleeing before the mighty Pharaoh's host.

Jonathan Mitchel Sewall thought Washington morally superior to Moses, since he only lost his temper once, at Monmouth, while Moses was "provoked to act with rashness at Sinai's base, and once to speak unadvisedly at the rock of Oreb" (*Eulogies* 39). After Washington wrote his first farewell address, to the state governors on resigning his war powers, a New Englander thought of the Twelve Tribes: "When I read General Washington's circular letter

I imagine myself in the presence of the Great General of the twelve United States of Israel" (Freeman 5.446).

Jedidiah Morse, preaching at Charlestown, Massachusetts, composed what amounts to a long dissertation on the parallels between the life of Moses and that of Washington.

Destined to act in the double capacity of a General and a Lawgiver to the tribes of Israel, to be at the same time (under God) their deliverer from Egyptian bondage, their conductor by a most difficult and wondrous way to the promised land, the dispenser of wise and excellent laws for their internal regulation, and the instrument of their exaltation to independence and glory among the nations, God in his wisdom was pleased to order the events of his life in a manner wisely suited to prepare him for his various and important offices.

Ten pages are devoted to Moses' career "as a General, a Statesman, and a Man." Then Washington is introduced, to run the same course.

Never, perhaps, were coincidences in character and fortune, between any two illustrious men who have lived, so numerous and striking as between Moses and Washington. If the latter selected Moses as his model, he was certainly wise in his choice and happy in his imitation. Both were born for great and similar achievements—to deliver under the guidance of providence, each the tribes of their respective countrymen, from the yoke of oppression, and to establish them (with the best form of government and the wisest code of laws) an independent and respectable nation.

Did Moses serve with the Egyptians against Ethiopians? So did Washington serve with Braddock against Indians. Did Moses retire from military life to keep sheep? So did Washington return to agriculture. Each was chosen to lead, to institute law, to deliver his people.

By 1800 the Mosaic comparison was everywhere—there was nothing surprising in that. But after 1800 it fades rapidly toward almost entire disappearance—which *is* surprising. And this fall-off in the verbal comparison draws attention to an interesting omission: The visual arts never showed Washington as Moses. He could be released to heaven by Father Time with his forelock (Figure 6), but not by Moses with his horns of light. When we consider the other visual symbols marshaled around the figure of Washington, this fact suggests Holmes's famous clue, the dog that did not bark.

Even before 1800, people had expressed some misgivings about the Moses comparison. Moses, after all, did not enter the Promised Land, whereas Washington dwelt from the outset in the land he finally ruled after liberating it. This had important consequences. It was one thing for preachers to think of Washington as their deliverer from King George's Egypt. But when the people were no longer escaping a ruler or fleeing *toward* a realm, the Mosaic dispensation had some troubling aspects. American laws were hammered out in convention at Philadelphia, not delivered down from God's mountain. The threat in the latter form of legislation was made clear by the few men (like David Austin) who called for a theocracy modeled on ancient Israel's.

One way to handle the theocratic premise of Mosaic rule was to secularize one's picture of Moses—a tendency manifest in all references to his "legislation." The accent is put on human prudence rather than divine inspiration. The long treatment of Moses by Jedidiah Morse emphasized this. Moses is providentially equipped to rule by the experiences he undergoes, making him a statesman (22). Providence, guiding all events, allows for this formation, but does not effect it by divine intervention. There is no burning bush in this tale of a secular Moses. Washington advances in prudence by modeling himself on the Mosaic heroism (30), not by sharing a theophany with Moses.

There is an obvious problem with this treatment of the Moses image. If it can be sanitized, made safe, only by a process of secularization, why not go all the way and choose an entirely secular model? This is in fact what happened. Classical models drove out biblical ones in the important first decade after Washington's death, the period when Weems and others fixed the image of the hero. Washington could be so easily "bourgeoisified" by the Victorian age, by McGuffey's Readers, precisely because he had been secularized, brought down from heaven, in the first stage of his cult.

A key figure in the stabilizing of Washington's secular image was, ironically, a man who made his living in large part by selling Bibles (as well as preaching from them). Mason Locke Weems published his first short edition of the *Life of Washington* in 1800, the year when many eulogists were recalling the wartime Moses comparison. Yet there is only one casual reference to Moses in Weems's eighty pages. Washington is praised as a legislator because, like Moses, Lycurgus, and Numa, he encouraged respect for religion (30)—two classical leaders are mentioned for the one Jewish hero. In the expanded final edition of his work, Weems added one more reference to Moses, saying Washington died alone "like Moses alone on the top of Pisgah" (166). There is no mention of the Revolution as a passage out of Egyptian power, the moral point of most comparisons with Moses. When Weems's Washington crosses the Delaware, he does it with classical references to the Rubicon, not Mosaic references to the Red Sea (83).

The first edition of the biography had a classical litany that Weems would use as his guide in creating the final picture:

Washington was pious as Numa, just as Aristides, temperate as Epictetus, patriotic as Regulus. In giving public trusts, impartial as Severus; in victory, modest as Scipio—prudent as Fabius, rapid as Marcellus, undaunted as Hannibal, as Cincinnatus disinterested, to liberty firm as Cato, and respectful of the laws as Socrates (72).

The popularity of Weems's work shows that this secularizing effort was acceptable to a mass audience. Whether Weems found the tendency in his customers, or just found he could instill it, he certainly advanced it. While "Connecticut Wits" like Timothy Dwight were still treating Washington as another Moses, Weems had settled on the principal model for Washington's specific virtue: Cincinnatus.

The values to be instilled by his biography animate the address Weems gave in 1802, "The True Patriot":

Of this sort was that glory of Rome . . . and of all republican virtue, Cincinnatus, the proprietor of only four acres of ground. The Equi and the Volsci, two warlike nations uniting all their forces, burst into the Roman territories like a resistless cataract, sweeping everything before them. Blank with terror, the Romans sent for Cincinnatus to hasten to the command of their little army and play the last stake for his trembling countrymen. They found the hero at his plough. Having unyoked his oxen he hastened to the army—who, at his appearance, felt as did our troubled fathers in 1774 [sic] when the godlike figure of Washington stood before them on the plains of Boston to fight the battles of liberty. In two days he brought the Romans in sight of the combined armies; he formed his line of battle and, after reminding them what they were to fight for, he led them on to the charge with such resistless impetuosity that he obtained a complete victory and gave, as it were, a new life to his country's liberties. Soon as this great work was done, he took an affectionate leave of his gallant army and returned to cultivate his four acres with the same hands which had so gloriously defended the liberties of his country (43–44).

In the biography, Weems made Cincinnatus the symbolic center of a prophetic dream that comes to Washington's mother. This meant he had to face a problem involved in the summons from the plow—one that could be evaded by those who did not *visualize* the symbol in a concrete setting. Only slaves plowed on the great plantations. There is no evidence that Jefferson (for instance) ever put his hand to the plow he invented. Weems solved this problem with some ingenuity:

George, at that time about five years old, was in the garden with his corn-stalk plow, busily running little furrows in the sand, in imitation of Negro Dick, a fine black boy with whose plowing George was so taken that it was sometimes a hard matter to get him to his dinner. And so, as I [Washington's mother is speaking] was sitting in the piazza at my work,

I suddenly heard in my dream a kind of roaring noise on the eastern side of the house. On running out to see what was the matter, I beheld a dreadful sheet of fire bursting from the roof. The sight struck me with a horror which took away my strength, and threw me almost senseless to the ground. My husband and the servants, as I saw in my dream, soon came up; but, like myself, were so terrified at the sight that they could make no attempt to extinguish the flames. In this most distressing state, the image of my little son came (I thought) to my mind more dear and tender than ever, and turning towards the garden where he was engaged with his little corn-stalk plow, I screamed out twice with all my might, "George! George!" In a moment, as I thought, he threw down his mimic plow and came running . . .

The fire is only put out when Benjamin Franklin appears with a French *chabot* (symbol of French naval power) from which George pours the water that puts out the flames.

Those who mock Weems as a pious biographer have mistaken his genre. A dream symbol like that of Cincinnatus shows that his work should not be compared with, say, Marshall's *Life of Washington,* but with Dwight's *Conquest of Canaan* or Barlow's *Columbiad*. Weems gives us the meaning of Washington in a set of symbols, not following narrative logic at all. He was not recording events, but fashioning an icon. And Weems's book not only found more readers than the stilted epics from Connecticut did; it had more, and more truthful, things to tell those readers.

PLATE I   Charles Willson Peale, *Washington at the Battle of Princeton*
. . . phoenix from death's ashes

PLATE 3   John Trumbull,
General Washington at Verplanck's Point (1790)
. . . officer on a call

PLATE 5   Gilbert Stuart, Lansdowne portrait of Washington (1796)
. . . "Fellow citizens . . ."

PLATE 6   Jean-Antoine Houdon, Richmond statue of Washington
. . . metamorphosis to citizen

IV

WEEMS AND THE CHERRY TREE

To copy out our father's bright example.
—Addison, *Cato* 1.1

EVERYONE NOTICES, of course, the blatant pictorial reference in Grant Wood's *Parson Weems' Fable,* the reference to Gilbert Stuart's Athenaeum portrait—the head of a President in his sixties stuck on the body of a boy (Figure 1). The joke is double-edged if we remember that Stuart himself stuck the Athenaeum head on various models' bodies, as products of his Washington industry (see the Lansdowne portrait, Plate 5). Wood is saying that the Weems child is no child at all, but an ageless demi-human sent, like Mark Twain's Franklin, to blight playgrounds with adult counsel. He is an infiltrator from a parsonical world. The Weems who stands offstage is pulling the puppet's strings. Not a lofty view of Washington. And not, I shall be arguing, Weems's own view.

There is another side of Wood's picture too—one reflected in a less-noticed pictorial reference. The scene of a showman pulling back the curtain is taken from Charles Willson Peale's famous

7   Charles Willson Peale, *The Artist in His Museum* (1822)
. . . the outside brought inside, and sorted

painting of his own museum in Philadelphia (Figure 7).* Peale tried to classify the riches of American natural life, species by species, in the cases lit behind his tasseled curtain. Like Jefferson decorating his hallway with the finds of western exploration, Peale has domesticated nature, tamed it with scientific tools (beginning with his taxidermy kit, in the left foreground). To the right, we are teased with a glimpse of the great *Incognitum Americanum,* the mastodon Peale excavated. The woman in the middle distance, who sees what we cannot, is rapt with wonder.

Wood reverses Peale's world. The latter brings nature inside. Wood takes artifice outside—Washington's tree grows out of a carpet, lit by a stage "spotlight." The tassels on Wood's curtain are little cherries, as artificial as the ones hung on the tree. Peale introduces us to nature and the real; Wood opens the curtain on an imagined America that is reduced to one cherished lie—that the Father of his Country could not lie. Wood directs his mild satire at the admirers of Stuart who abandoned Peale's reality for Weems's fairy tale. But in fact the joke may be on Wood. Weems stood much closer to Peale in his outlook than to the world Wood foists on him.

Weems wanted to domesticate the classics, to categorize the natural. His pages, like Peale's museum, are full of authentic American life. The Homeric simile had been introduced to American literature by the Connecticut Wits, writing their dreary epics about the Revolution. None of them gives a truly American version of the ancient passages. But Weems does. Here is Homer's death of Sarpedon applied, under American skies, to the agony of Tarleton's troops:

---

*There is, in fact, a third reference in Wood's witty picture. The circle of pointing fingers recalls Thomas Nast's famous cartoon of mutually blaming politicians ("Who Stole the People's Money?"). George is asking the hatchet to "take the rap"—but *it* closes the circle by pointing back to Weems, who is responsible for inventing the whole legend.

The ground was covered with the dead; the tops of the aged pines shook with the ascending ghosts. With feeble cries and groans, at once they rose like flocks of snow-white swans when the cold blasts strike them on the lakes of Canada and send them on widespread wings far to the south to seek a happier clime (*Life of Washington,* ch. 10).

Weems was as interested in the American mammoth as Jefferson and Peale were—and as convinced that it was still extant, since no link could fall out of "the chain of being." Weems was sure the beast could be found alive in Missouri:

As when a mammoth suddenly dashes in among a thousand buffaloes, feeding at large on the vast plains of Missouri; all at once the innumerous herd, with wildly rolling eyes and hideous bellowings, break forth into flight, while close at their heels, the roaring monster follows—earth trembles as they fly. Such was the noise in the chase of Tarleton, when the swords of Washington's cavalry pursued his troops from Cowpens' famous fields (ibid.).

There is a vitality here, a combination of literary love and native observation, that is paralleled in William Rush's energetic American eagles. Rush, who collaborated with Peale on his museums, twisted one eagle into human agonies (Figure 8)—an anthropomorphic achievement explained by the fact that the Pennsylvania Academy had a cast of the Laocoon in its collection (Figure 9). Like Rush, Weems was quirkily learned; his naïveté is deliberate—an attempt to reach a popular audience with precisely the classical ideals the Connecticut Wits embalmed in dead books. Weems's books live—especially his *Washington.*

For Washington's future celebrant, Weems showed little interest in serving under him. After leaving America to study medicine in Scotland, he returned during the Revolution, and—at a time when this would raise suspicions of loyalty to the British crown as well as church—studied to become an Anglican priest. His ministry in America was rather aimless until, in 1793, he real-

8   William Rush, *Eagle* (c. 1810)
. . . eagle agonistes

ized that selling Bibles was a way of making a living as well as
preaching the gospel. Grandly he commenced, in his term, "bibli-
opolist"—made himself a type of that American salesman who links
God with gain: "Thank God, the Bible still goes well. I am *agreeably surprised* to find among the multitude such a spirit of veneration for the Bible. Good old Book! I hope we shall live by you in
this world and in the world to come!" A brisk trade was now his
mission in life, and business setbacks weighed down his mono-
syllables, like sins oppressing the prophets: "God knows there is

9   Hellenistic Period, *Laocoon*
         . . . struggling to be free

nothing I so dread as *Dead stock, dull* sales, back *loads,* and *blank looks.*" It is the salesman's eternal lament, followed by words that skip and sing: "But the Joy of my soul is quick and clean sales — heavy pockets, and light hearts."

Weems traveled Maryland and the South, drawing most of his supplies from the important Irish publisher in Philadelphia, Matthew Carey. The two men traded hopes and curses, in a comic marriage of endless wrangling. The Parson accused the Catholic of undermining sales of the Bible. Shipping problems led to pseudo-Ciceronian denunciation: "Quotuscunque Catalina! how long, thou eldest born of confusion, how long wilt thou continue to send the *books* to South James River, and the *invoice* to the head waters of Patomack?"

Weems saw himself as a hero of bibliopoly being undercut by his field commander:

If you knew all, if you knew the globules of rich sweat I have lost, the tears of grief and vexation I have shed in consequence of your ill treat-ment of me, your oppressing and crushing me to the earth by ten thou-sand puritanical books which as a good Catholic you know I did not request you to send, nay, was eternally remonstrating against your send-ing, representing them to you as unsaleable in this State as Fiddles at a Conventicle . . . I deem it glory to circulate valuable books. I would circulate millions. This cannot be effected without the character of *cheap-ness.* Let but the public point to me and say *"there goes the little Parson that brings us so many clever books and so cheap,"* and I ask no more. But this building a high fortune on low priced books, appears to you strange as the fatn'ing a Calf by bleeding it. But the Scotch Merchants, who are your best marksmen at a dollar on the wing, will tell you that there's nothing like the nimble ninepence.

Any doubt about his dedication and competence led to Micawber eloquence:

The style of your last letter was so pathetically keen that it made a scratch on my pericardium, though cased in well-tempered innocence. Superior to retaliation, I haste to answer your epistle and to develop my plan of past conduct . . . There is a capriciousness in your character and conduct which will forever embitter the soul, and curse the existence of

—M. L. Weems

[P.S.] Lugging about a heavy book with light profits and long expenditures, and after all not allowed to eat my poor solitary crust in peace, is enough to make me wish I had been born a butcher's dog and not a poor dependent on your smiles.

When a rival beat Carey to the production of a particular Bible, Weems felt heroism drain from him, having lost its nutriment of fame:

Why, I would ask, why rose the steel of Brutus against the life of Caesar? Had Caesar wronged Brutus of that *trash,* his purse? No—not to the value of an obolus. But Caesar had wronged Brutus of that which generous minds hold dearer than gold—he had wronged him of his *Equality &c,* so though you never wronged me of my gold, yet you have wronged me of my well-earned fame. From the moment I commenced the glorious toils of a Bookseller, I coveted the honor of circulating a Family bible.

Weems's words nimbly follow his dragonflying moods. He gives a vitality to everything he touches. The prophets and poets are summoned to his aid—with appropriate updating: "Some men asking for bread have been complimented with a brickbat." The prose is so vibrant it makes the book quiver in your hand. Weems was not a great writer, but he was a great letter writer. His masterpiece was composed without his noticing; and it was not published till 1928, when Emily Skeel brought out the letters patiently collected by her brother, Paul Leicester Ford. A man springs from these pages as from the great eighteenth-century diaries, Boswell's or Walpole's.

Though Weems strove for a more dignified carriage in the books he wrote for publication, something of his letters' dash and enthusiasm is evident there as well. Surely no one ever preached in a more swashbuckling way the evils of dueling: "The next morning would have seen him on the field, and, in language lately heard in this state, calling out to his hated antagonist, *You have injured me, sir, beyond reconciliation, and by God, I'll kill you if I can.* While his antagonist, in a style equally musical and Christian, rejoins, *Kill and be damned!* Pop go the pistols—down tumbles one of the combatants; while the murderer with knocking knees and looks of Cain, flies from the avenger of blood!" (*Life of Washington,* 189–90). Before movies and television, that was as vivid a "shoot-out" as one could get, short of the real thing.

There is a cinematic vigor, too, in the picture of the beaten English finally leaving New York Harbor: "Then all in a moment they fly to work. Some, seizing the ready handspikes, vault high upon the windlasses, thence coming down all at once with the Yo-heave-O, they shake the sounding decks and tear from their dark cozy beds the ponderous anchors. Others, with halyards hard strained through the creaking blocks, sway aloft the wide-extended yards, and spread their canvas to the gale, which, with increasing freshness, bears the broad-winged ships in foam and thunder through the waves" (*Life of Washington,* 114–15).

If his prose was always more lively than dignified, Weems's causes were good ones, ardently promoted, courageously disseminated. Weems was a natural educator, who advocated school for girls as well as boys and hated the schoolmaster's rod. And while there is no questioning his rather frothy sincerity, the preacher was not a prude. After writing a tract that defended premarital chastity and calling it *Hymen's Recruit,* Weems complained when the book was badly packed for shipping: "The Hymens [are] so rammed and jammed that I'm sure the nests of Love will hardly ever again be got into shipshape."

A Billy Graham or Fulton Sheen would later use radio and TV in commercially successful ways. But Weems had first to create his medium, and even his audience, before the selling began. He trudged from church to church, fair to fair, going straight from the pulpit to his book cart, or waiting for cockfights to break up. He was a market sampler, an author's agent, a publisher's scout.

He tested products, varied them, repackaged them. The final edition of his *Life of Washington* grew, in part, from unsuccessful attempts to sell John Marshall's ponderous five volumes on the subject.

The Bible remained the basis of Weems's business; but he knew there must be different models for different markets: "I tell you this is the very season and age of the Bible, Bible Dictionaries, Bible tales, Bible stories—Bibles plain or paraphrased, Carey's Bibles, Collins' Bibles, Clarke's Bibles, Kimptor's Bibles, no matter what or whose, all, all will go down—so wide is the crater of public appetite at this time. God be thanked for it." He would cram Bibles down the national maw; he would *force* America to read—and, in large part, he did.

All this vigor of writing was devoted to causes of the Enlightenment. He opposed slavery, dueling, gambling, tobacco, and alcohol in a South devoted to all these items. But his main cause was religious toleration. Weems was notoriously latitudinarian in his theology; he would preach in any denomination's pulpit, and praise any sincere theism (even Franklin's nonpracticing kind). In all four of his biographies, a constant theme is the importance of religious tolerance.

Admittedly, this message was unavoidable in the biography of a man who had become the very symbol of tolerance, William Penn. But Weems goes to what his age would have thought extremes of tolerance. He even honors the Indians' religion, almost universally dismissed as idolatry by "civilized" Americans (ch. 17). Penn's father is ridiculed as a type of intolerance for not supporting his son's new vision (ch. 13). That vision is presented as superior to earlier forms of religion precisely because it escaped the sophistries of quibbling theologians.

If this moral was to be expected in a life of Penn, it is not what most readers would anticipate when picking up the story of General Francis Marion, the "Swamp Fox" (1810). Yet here, too,

Weems ridicules an ancestor—a great-grandfather in Marion's case; not, as with Penn, the hero's father—for narrow-mindedness. This ancestor "was of that sort who place all their religion in forms and notions, [who] could smile and look very fond upon a man, though not overmoral, provided that man went to his church" (ch. 1). America, Weems argues, profited by the French intolerance that drove Marion's Huguenot parents to the New World. And Marion himself is depicted as a friend of dissenting sects: "Hearing one of his friends say that the methodists and baptists were progressing rapidly in some parts of the state, he replied, 'Well, thank God for that; that is good news.' The same gentleman then asked him what he thought was the best religion. 'I know but one religion,' he answered, 'and that is hearty love of God and man' " (ch. 32).

The real test of Weems's tolerance was bound to be the life of Franklin (1815). Franklin's ancestors, too, are made the victims of religious persecution (ch. 2). Weems gives the best debating points to young Benjamin when he questions his father's orthodoxy (ch. 17). The hero attacks church attendance with an argument from the subject's own *Autobiography:* "I hardly ever hear anything but lean chaffy discourse about the trinity and baptism and elections and reprobations and final perseverances and covenants and a thousand other such things which do not strike my fancy as religion at all, because not in the least calculated, as I think, to sweeten and ennoble men's natures and make them love and do good to one another." Franklin wanders from theism (ch. 23), but returns to it when he sees atheism's practical fruits (ch. 26). Since he held that virtue is men's only true happiness (ch. 32), he lived the gospel without having to preach it (ch. 43).

Weems's life of Washington (1808) has the same themes as the later biographies. Here, too, Weems teaches religious tolerance, but indirectly. The first virtue given Washington in the chapter that begins consideration of his character (ch. 13) is, as one would expect, religion. Washington is ranked with the great heroes who were exemplary in their regard for and protection of religion. Only one of these heroes is a Christian, and that one a Catholic (Cortez). One is a Jew—and *not* Moses: Jacob. The other four are classical models: Epaminondas, Socrates, Scipio, and Marcus Aurelius. (In the first version of the life, in 1800, the only parallel given for Washington in this place was Epaminondas, on page 25.) On the other hand, all the exemplars of irreligious behavior, the men contrasted with Washington, are evil Christians: Benedict Arnold, Charles Lee, Alexander Hamilton, and Aaron Burr. (Hamilton is included because he consented to a duel, a great sin in the Weems program of reform.)

It will be seen that Weems's emphasis throughout is on public virtue and civic duty, the kind of religion Franklin and Rousseau would support, and Weems stresses the *practical* fruits of this religion in Washington's career. Even the most famous story of private piety, the prayer at Valley Forge, is adduced to support civic duty. The Quaker of the story, after seeing Washington pray, tells his wife: "Thee knows that I always thought the sword and the gospel utterly inconsistent; and that no man could be a soldier and a Christian at the same time. But George Washington has this day convinced me of my mistake." Washington's virtue reaches across denominational boundaries to assure men of the justice of his cause. Weems is praising an "enlightened," eighteenth-century religion, whose point a modern scholar can miss if he is predisposed to dismiss Weems. Weems tells a "conversion story"—but the conversion is not to religion (his Potts is already religious); it is to *political* duty.

Douglas Southall Freeman proved that Weems did not invent his famous story of the old man who clubbed Washington in a tavern. This seems to fit all too pat Weems's campaign against duels. But the interesting thing is that Washington lived up to that code in fact—as he did to the ideal of freeing his slaves. What is even more important, the tavern story occurs in the chapter Weems devoted to Washington's benevolence—the eighteenth-century virtue of enlightened men which Weems puts next after public religion.

Even the most naïve stories in Weems have an enlightened background or purpose. Washington's father, to demonstrate the difference between accident and causality, plants cabbage seeds in the form of George's name, tries to pass off the result, lets George see through the ruse, then argues from the more complex design of the universe to a divine "planter." It has long been known that Weems took this story from the Scottish philosopher James Beattie, who actually performed this experiment with his child "to make a trial how far his own reason could go in tracing out" the principle of causality.

Beattie, praised by Dr. Johnson, was among those Scots who advocated more liberal educational methods for children. Most Scottish philosophers after Francis Hutcheson believed in a common moral sense and natural benevolence; this made them trust nature rather than the rod and throw off Calvinist notions of child care. John Gregory, who taught the teacher of Thomas Jefferson, wrote a book that was the Dr. Spock manual of its day (1765), *A Comparative View of the State and Faculties of Man With Those of the Animal World*. If animals learn by instinct and experiment, so should humans. They need the stimulation of curiosity, not rote repetition under threat. It was the kind of reform Rousseau preached in *Émile*.

Weems tells the cabbage story in the chapter devoted to praise of Washington's father as an educator: "Never did the wise Ulysses take more pain with his beloved Telemachus than did Mr. Washington with George." Even here Weems is secularizing. Marcus Cunliffe notes that other biographers stressed George's devotion to his *mother*, creating a kind of Holy Family in the education scenes (xxxix–xl). Weems not only makes the father the instructor; he compares him to a classical hero preparing his son for a public career.

In his other biographies, Weems praised parents for the stimulation of a child's own reasoning power. He borrows certain emphases from Franklin's *Autobiography*. Franklin's father uses mealtimes to stimulate Ben's mind (ch. 4), takes him to craftsmen's shops to let him see how things are actually made (ch. 5), and lets Ben discover his own lack of poetical gifts simply by putting a volume of Pope where he would pick it up (ch. 7). Penn's mother instructs William in the difference between accident and causality in a way similar to Washington père's, asking how human nourishment could in all its ramifications take place by accident—"how his milk and bread, white as snow, should be turned into blood red as crimson; and how that blood soft as milk should be turned, some into sweet little teeth, white and hard as ivory; and some into soft flowing hair, like silk; some into sweet polished cheeks, like rose buds; and some into bright shining eyes, like diamonds."

Ah, but what of the cherry tree? Do we not, in that famous story, descend to Weems at his simple-moralizing worst? Not in the original. In the McGuffey Readers and elsewhere, the tale takes on a form altered as well as truncated, with its simple moral aimed at children: "Never tell a lie." But that is not Weems's point. His anecdote occurs in the chapter that praises Washington's father as another Ulysses, and it has a long prologue. George has asked his father if he ever tells lies. The father answers with good permissive doctrine of the Gregory sort:

At least you shall never, from me, have cause to be guilty of so shameful a thing. Many parents, indeed, even compel their children to this vile practice, by barbarously berating them for every little fault; hence, on the next offence, the little terrified creature slips out a lie just to escape the rod. But as to yourself, George, you know I have always told you, and now tell you again, that whenever by accident you do anything wrong—which must often be the case, as you are but a poor little boy yet, without experience or knowledge—never tell a falsehood to conceal it; but come bravely up, my son, like a little man, and tell me of it and, instead of beating you, George, I will but the more honor and love you for it, my dear.

Even the terms of endearment are part of the Weems message on treatment of children.

After the child, with one unconsidered stroke, "barks" the "beautiful young English cherry tree," he is able to tell the truth because his parent has not terrified him with fear. And the conclusion of the tale makes it clear that the hero is Washington's father:

"Run to my arms, you dearest boy," cried his father in transports, "run to my arms. Glad am I, George, that you killed my tree; for you have paid me for it a thousandfold. Such an act of heroism in my son is worth more than a thousand trees, though blossomed with silver and their fruits of purest gold." It was in this way, by interesting at once both his heart and head, that Mr. Washington conducted George with great ease and pleasure along the happy paths of virtue.

In Weems, all the exaggeration is of affection, *calling* the boy a hero, and so *making* him one. Praise is the proper stimulant of virtue. The moral is directed at the parents.

In McGuffey's retelling of the story, for the *New Third Reader,* the exaggeration is all of denunciation, depicting the viciousness of lying. No mention is made of parental fondness as a deterrent to lies. Indeed, the father forewarns his son in this grisly way: "Oh George, rather than see you come to this [lying], dear as you are to me, gladly would I assist to nail you up in your little coffin, and follow you to your grave." If that did not make a liar of the boy, nothing would. The threats, the assaults on the boy's emotions, are piled up with glee; the father talks of "giving him up" if George ever lies. We have moved from the world of humane enlightenment to morbid Victorian preoccupation with death. Young George is made to sleep under the shadow of a coffin, like Oliver Twist at Mr. Sowerberry's. It is a long trip from the world of Cincinnatus to that of Little Nell. Yet Weems's Washington cannot be understood apart from the image of Cincinnatus. Nor, as we shall see, can Greenough's Washington.

10 Jean-Auguste-Dominique Ingres, *Jupiter and Thetis* (1811)
. . . the angry eagle of disrupted order

V

GREENOUGH AND PHEIDIAS

> To strike thee dumb, turn up thy eyes to Cato!
> There may'st thou see to what a godlike height
> The Roman virtues lift up mortal man.
> —Addison, *Cato* 1.4

SCULPTING HIS WASHINGTON for the Capitol Rotunda (Figure 2), Horatio Greenough took for his model what the neoclassical period believed was the greatest statue ever created, by the greatest sculptor who ever lived—the Elian Zeus of Pheidias. Since that chryselephantine wonder was no longer extant, artists had to rely on the description given by Pausanias, and on coins of Elis that celebrated the work. Here is what Pausanias had to say (5.11):

The seated god is himself fashioned from gold and ivory; the garland on his head appears to be real olive shoots. In his right hand he holds a Victory, also of gold and ivory, offering a ribbon, a garland on her head. In the god's left hand there is a sceptre, encrusted with every kind of metal, and the bird on the tip is an eagle.

There were many attempts to invoke the great image. Ingres made the effort in 1811 with his *Jupiter and Thetis* (Figure 10). His principal departure from the ancient design is a shift of the scepter from the god's left hand to his right. The reason for the change should be evident. The original statue showed Zeus conferring on the Elians their victory against Pisa (Pausanias 5.10). The right hand was the proper one for conferring gifts or greetings, from the time of Homer's *Iliad* (24.283–84) and *Odyssey* (1.120–21). But in the painting by Ingres, Thetis is begging for what cannot be, for the life of her doomed son, Achilles. The shift of the scepter, the closing round it of the giving hand, precludes any favorable response. Zeus is the ruler of Destiny here, unbending as the rod he lifts against Thetis' supple entreaty. Thetis is trying to reverse the fixed order of things, over which Jupiter presides. This explains the resentful gaze of the eagle, which has been displaced from the god's executing right hand. Thetis is "out of her place," literally, in making such a request.

The shifting of the scepter shows a sensitivity, on Ingres's part, to the symbolism of the original, which saw the right-hand side as the source of action, either to give or to refuse. For Aristotle, all motion originated from the right, in the heavens as well as in man's body. It was a maxim of Greek medical literature— passed down from Parmenides to Aristotle and Galen—that the right side of the human body was more male than the left side: "Right, male; left, female." In terms of vitality and power, Aristotle claimed, "the right side has the Right" (*De Incessu* 706a21– 22).

This convention was, if anything, strengthened in Christian art, which illustrated scriptural references to the right side as that of the saved or the privileged. In Pauline texts, God placed Jesus at his right hand. In Last Judgments, the right hand summons the saved to rise. In *sacre conversazioni,* the favored saint or patron was put at the Virgin's right hand. Charles Singleton, in his edition of Dante (*Inferno* 1.30), traced the way this "right hand" theology could be extended to the right foot:

A long tradition applied the metaphor of feet to faculties of the soul. As this metaphor merged with Aristotle's dictum that all motion originates from the right, it was said the first step is taken by the right foot while the left remains stationary. The left foot was seen as the *pes firmior,* the

11   Albrecht Dürer, *Adam and Eve* (1504)
. . . the wrong hands

12   Studio of Jacques-Louis David, Toledo *Oath of the Horatii* (1786)
    . . . swords brought forward, plow recessed

firmer or less "agile." Later, in Christian tradition, there came about a
more specific identification of the "two feet of the soul." According to
Bonaventura and others, the "foot" or power that moves first is the *ap-
prehensivus,* or the intellect, and therefore is the right. The other or left
"foot" is the *affectus* or *appetitivus*—i.e., the will. In Adam's sin, wherein
all men sinned, it was the intellect or right "foot" that suffered the wound
of ignorance, while the left "foot," the *affectus* or will—the *pes firmior*—
suffered the wound of concupiscence. As a result, postlapsarian man is a
limping creature (*homo claudus*). He limps especially in his *left* foot, because it is wounded by concupiscence, the chief *vulneratio* of original sin.
In this opening scene of the poem, the wayfarer, as he strives to climb
toward the light at the summit, has to discover that he bears within him
the weakness of *homo claudus.* He can see the light at the summit (seeing,
in this case, is a function of the intellect or right "foot"). At best, however, he can only limp toward the light he sees, because in his other

58

13   Jean-Jacques Hauer, *Lafayette and Madame Roland* (c. 1791)
. . . thinkers on the right, men of action on the left

power, his will—the left "foot" or *pes firmior*—he bears the wound of concupiscence.

This theological symbolism is carefully worked out in Dürer's 1504 *Adam and Eve* (Figure 11), where Adam steps forward on his left (sinful) foot to take the apple with his left hand. What should be the *pes firmior* is moved by the concupiscence that will ever after cripple it. By contrast, the side of Adam's body that should be active rests in a "sleep of reason," signified by the right arm's dependence on the supporting branch. In Eve, that order is reversed: since she should be the passive and obedient partner, her sin is accomplished by an "unnatural" assertiveness in the right hand, which takes the apple. Adam has abdicated his rightful rule to Eve—with the resulting "fall" suggested by the vertiginous perch of the mountain goat in the top right corner of the picture.

Of course, the right-hand side of a character within a picture is on the viewer's *left*-hand side. As every actor must learn, "stage right" is the audience's left—just as, in heraldry, the "dexter" quarter is on the viewer's left. This explains the division of such pictures as Dürer's *Adam and Eve* into a "male left, female right" scheme. David's Horatii, unlike Dürer's Adam, stride forward on their right feet, raising their right hands in the oath taken on their swords, all martial energy and manly control, while the female side of the picture is reserved for grieving collapse and exhaustion (Figure 12).

This division is exploitable even when the artist wants to stress the *complementarity* of the "male" and "female" sides of his picture. Jean-Jacques Hauer's painting known as *Lafayette and Madame Roland Drawing a Plan for the Festival of the Federation* (Figure 13) arranges the busts behind the male and female figures with men of *action* on the left (Mirabeau and the soldier Desilles), men of *thought* on the right (Franklin and Rousseau). The male figure's military uniform is contrasted with the domestic musical instruments on the right side—though even these are at the service of the revolution, since the "Ça Ira" is on the music stand. Power

14   John Trumbull, *The Surrender of Lord Cornwallis at Yorktown*
(1787–c. 1828)
     . . . British yield to a Washington yielding his place

and culture are joined here, the male military effort and the "female" arts of education.

As the Hauer painting shows, the right side of the picture need not be ignoble. In fact, Washington expresses his nobility in Trumbull's *Resignation* (Figure 5) by returning his commission to the political *left* side of the painting, with its high pediment and raised platform of the civil power, so that he may return to the domestic world of the picture's *right* side, with its lower lintel, under which Washington will pass to his farm.

Since Trumbull thought in terms of left and right as the active and the passive sides of his paintings, his surrender scenes put the victors on the right to *receive* capitulation—see *The Surrender of Lord Cornwallis at Yorktown* (Figure 14), as well as the reception of the German officer's submission in *The Capture of the Hessians at Trenton*. The left side of the body (viewer's right) is easily as-

15   Jacques-Louis David, *Paris and Helen* (1788)
. . . self-disarmed

sociated with compassion, since that is where the heart is. Aristotle
thought the heart's presence there was compensatory, to help the
"weak" side of the body (*De Partibus* 66b7–11).

Of course, this formula of neoclassical art is only effective when
it is used in a nonformulaic way. Ingres, for instance, brought it
to life by putting Thetis on the wrong side of his picture (Figure
10), suggesting a disruption in the very nature of things. David
achieves the same effect by putting the *male* on the wrong side. In
his *Paris and Helen* (Figure 15), Paris has left his weapons hanging
on the left side of the picture, crossed over into female territory,
and taken up the lyre. He has forsaken the war he caused, to enjoy
the soft delights of the woman he caused it for. This desertion of
the heroic order stands in stark contrast to the heroic death of
Paris' brother (Figure 16), whose arm (spanning the left side of

16   Jacques-Louis David, *Andromache Mourning Hector* (1785)
. . . a quintet of dead and living hands

17 Jacques-Louis David, *Napoleon Distributing the Eagles*
. . . as if filmed by Leni Riefenstahl

the picture) did not drop the sword until life was gone from it. Even in death Hector is given a victor's wreath, because he saved his honor. Andromache mourns on the right side of the picture, like her companions in sorrow of the *Brutus* and the *Horatii*.

Naturally, the power of the right hand was especially emphasized in pictures of rulers and deities—in, for instance, David's *Napoleon Distributing the Eagles* (Figure 17) or Ingres's *Portrait of Napoleon I on His Imperial Throne* (Figure 18). The latter picture resembles the *Jupiter and Thetis* (Figure 10). Like Jupiter in that painting, but unlike the Pheidian original, Napoleon has his right hand raised with the scepter. That is because Ingres has conflated two images here—the Greek statue of Zeus and seated images of Charlemagne. Napoleon is made to wield the eagle of antiquity *and* the scepter of French rule.

To find a Pheidian model with its *left* arm raised, we can look at Canova's statue of Napoleon as the god Mars (Figure 19). This

18 Jean-Auguste-Dominique Ingres, *Portrait of Napoleon I on His Imperial Throne* (1806)
. . . the fallen citizen

19   Antonio Canova, *Napoleon as the God Mars* (1811)
. . . by way of Pheidias' Zeus

20   Jacques-Louis David, *Death of Socrates* (1787)
. . . living in a reverence for death

is not a seated figure, but the upper torso is taken from Pheidias'
work, and the hands are in their original positions, the left raised
with a scepter, the right one bestowing a Victory.

David, too, kept the hands in their original position when he
imitated the Pheidian Zeus—but he removed the attributes from
both hands, and completely transformed the meaning of the pose.
In his *Socrates* (Figure 20), the philosopher's left hand is raised,
but not to hold a ruler's scepter; it indicates that higher law to
which man must submit. The right hand does not offer a Victory
but accepts death, taking the hemlock from the man who falters
at his task. Although the upper torso is in the Pheidian pose, the
right leg is lifted onto the bed where Socrates must lie. There is a
paradoxical freedom in this treatment of the lower body, emphasized by the fact that shackles have just been struck off Socrates'
ankles. Socrates, by his own choice, is a free man even in death—
the conqueror, not the conquered.

Greenough's Washington takes its place in this neoclassical

tradition of invoking Pheidias. Why, then, do people accept with awe the *Socrates* of 1787, but, half a century later, ridicule Greenough's statue? Part of the answer lies, of course, in that passage of time, a movement from the eighteenth century into the Victorian period. Admittedly, that time is partly spanned by works still looking back to Pheidias: Ingres's *Napoleon* in 1806, his *Jupiter and Thetis* in 1811, and Canova's *Napoleon* in 1811. Nonetheless, Greenough's statue was commissioned during Jackson's presidency and delivered during Tyler's. This almost guaranteed a prudish reaction to the bare-chested "Father of his Country." Perhaps if Trumbull had completed his apotheosis (Figure 21), the nudity would have been accepted. As late as 1821, Canova's statue of Washington, with bare legs and sandals, was given a warm reception in North Carolina (Figure 22).

By the 1840s, however, Greenough was dealing not only with changing tastes in the art world, but with an altered view of Washington, whose heroism had been shrunk by moralizing adulation. Then Nathaniel Hawthorne could write: "Did anybody ever see Washington naked? It is inconceivable. He has no nakedness, but I imagine was born with his clothes on and his hair powdered, and made a stately bow on his first appearance in the world." Hawthorne has already supplied Grant Wood with the program for his twentieth-century painting.

But the statue's nudity was not Greenough's only problem; not even his main problem. The work offended by its pomp and grandiosity. That is ironic, since Greenough thought he was fashioning an image of perfect humility. The statue is actually closer to David's *Socrates* than to the Pheidian original. Like Socrates, Greenough's Washington points to heaven with his raised hand, acknowledging the law man lives by. In this case, the right hand must be raised, since Washington's left hand returns his sword to the people, having completed his service to them. The right hand would offer the sword for *use*, in exhortation. The left hand must be used for surrender. Greenough's own intention was put in these

21   John Trumbull, study for *Apotheosis of Washington*
      . . . seized by heaven

22   Anonymous, *Lafayette Visiting Canova's Statue of Washington in 1824*
. . . the sword surrendered

23   Antonio Canova, *Theseus Having Slain the Minotaur* (1782)
      . . . the monster slain

words: "I have made him seated as first magistrate and he extends with his left hand the emblem of his military command toward the people as the sovereign. He points heavenward with his right hand. By this double gesture, my wish was to convey the idea of an entire abnegation of self."

It seems clear that Greenough was seeking purity and simplicity, not the bombastic quality most people find in the statue. He meant to have Washington enact the same surrender that Canova had, but without the paraphernalia and bustle of Canova's statue. Although the Canova work was destroyed when the capitol at Raleigh burnt down, we know it from models and from prints like the one that shows Lafayette visiting the statue in 1824. The sculptor has joined Washington's two great acts of surrender—the return of his commission after the war (symbolized in the Roman military garb and the sword laid down) and the departure from his presidency (shown in the Farewell Address he has begun, in Canova's translation, *"Al popolo degli Stati Uniti: Amici e concittadini"*). Canova took Washington's pose from his own early statue of Theseus resting after he slew the Minotaur (Figure 23). This was a particularly appropriate reference, since Plutarch says it was after the Minotaur episode that Theseus instituted the reign of law at Athens by putting aside his own royal power (35).

Canova's statue met with some criticism, but it was nothing like the storm of censure that broke around Greenough's work when it was lugged into the Capitol and almost broke the floor of the Rotunda. The objections were not to classicism as such, which was the dominant mode in American sculpture at the time. A reference to Pheidias would not be resented. Even William Rush, the native sculptor who had based his eagle on the Laocoon, carved a bust of Pheidias as the patron of Philadelphia's carvers and gilders in his triumphal chariot for the Grand Federal Procession to celebrate the ratification of the Constitution (Bantel 10). No, what was resented was not the sculptor but his subject, not Pheidias but Zeus. Despite the fussy classicism and exotic language of Canova,

24   Marguérite Gérard after Jean-Honoré Fragonard, *Eripuit Coelo* (1778)
. . . "He tore from heaven lightning . . ."

he was representing a man, a soldier. Greenough's Washington was meant to be a pure spirit, the embodiment of humility; but the scale and ideality of the thing make it superhuman. Though Greenough intended to re-create the spirit of Cincinnatus, he made the crucial mistake of dimming the secular nature of Washington's charisma, in ways that Weems never did. If Moses was unacceptable, finally, as a rounded expression of Washington's role, then Zeus had to be even less suitable.

The early representations of Washington are notable for their *lack* of divine attributes. The Enlightenment and early-nineteenth century had a taste for apotheosis, for heroes rapt up into heavens of abstraction. Yet, despite the immense regard expressed for Washington, he usually keeps his feet on the ground. Even Franklin, the "snuff-coloured Ben" of D. H. Lawrence, was treated more extravagantly by the artists than was the more stately Washington (Figures 24–26). The apparent exceptions to restraint in Washington's portraits help to establish the rule. Contrast, for instance, John Trumbull's sketch for an apotheosis of Washington (Figure 21) with a study by Ingres for a giant apotheosis of Napoleon (Figure 27). Napoleon's chariot is steered magically after the flight of Zeus's eagle, which bears the thunderbolt in its claws. The Emperor bears his royal insignia, and is being crowned a victor, while an angry spirit guards his throne against intruders. Trumbull's sketch, done in pencil and chalk on blue paper, shows us a man who rises by submission. He has no symbols of rank or office; his only gesture is one of humility. He is invited into the empyrean precisely because he does not storm it.

The only apotheosis of Washington that won popular favor was engraved by John J. Barralet (Figure 6), who stuck Gilbert Stuart's head on an all-purpose body, as Grant Wood would later do. Barralet loved visual symbols, and did much to popularize their use in America. He presents Washington's death as an intersection of time and eternity. Father Time, in the dark, bids farewell to Washington, assuring that his earthly reputation will be guarded;

25   Augustin Dupré, *The Genius of Franklin* (1784)
. . . and tore scepters from kings

26 Benjamin West, *Franklin Drawing Electricity from the Sky* (c. 1815)
. . . angels of the spheres domesticated

27　Jean-Auguste-Dominique Ingres, study for *Apotheosis of Napoleon* (1852)
　　　. . . seizing heaven

28 Gilbert Stuart, *George Washington*
. . . the Vaughan type, vulpine

while, in the light, an angel conducts him. The relation of the angel (higher, in light) to Father Time is repeated in the contrast between the three virtues and the more earthbound mourners before the tomb. Columbia and the native American look down, reflecting only on their loss, while Faith, like the eagle, looks up into the light. Hope clings to her anchor, which promises future stability, and Charity nurtures the young who will benefit from Washington's *exemplum virtutis,* his prowess in war (imaged by the Cincinnati eagle on the tomb) as in peace (indicated by the Masonic emblem). The earthbound eagle in Barralet's composition stands for the republic—this is not the tutelary bird of an individual genius, like Napoleon's eagle. Washington is seen, even here, within the context of his service to the republic. The long popularity of Barralet's design was proved when, after Lincoln's death, it was altered to show *his* reception into the political heavens.

Barralet's print, from the year of Washington's death, heralded the flood of "tomb-mourning" pictures to be found in American homes during the first half of the nineteenth century. The use of similar symbols for the departure of a loved member of the family demonstrates that this was a democratic genre, the apotheosis of everyman. Far from making outlandish claims about Washington, Barralet's work took his subject into the scene of domestic grieving, where he was indeed considered the "father" of his country.

The instinct for a secular and simple representation of Washington's heroism is nowhere better demonstrated than in the fact that the most popular portraits of all were the presidential portraits done by Gilbert Stuart—the vulpine Vaughan type (Figure 28), the avuncular Athenaeum type—where he appears simply as Citizen Washington, wearing the black suit of his inauguration, which the sardonic William Maclay mocked as "a second mourning" (*Diaries* 6.4–5). His favorite form of address, when speaking to his countrymen, whether as Commander in Chief or as President, was "my fellow citizens"; and the republic repaid this com-

29 John Trumbull, *Death of General Mercer at the Battle of Princeton* (1787–c. 1831)
. . . victory out of defeat

pliment by sensing that the highest recognition it could offer him was as a *citizen* leader. The man whose glory came from his return to the plow could gain no luster by mounting a throne or wearing a crown.

This ideal of citizen virtue is expressed in French political portraits from the early 1790s. But Napoleon brought back the imperial splendor realized in Ingres's portrait of 1806 (Figure 18). There, every conceivable sign of authority is made to adhere to Napoleon—earthly and heavenly, classical and Christian. The face is paled toward the ivory of Pheidias' Zeus. Napoleon treads on the Greek thunderbolt and the Roman eagle. The signs of the zodiac indicate that the stars in their courses fight for him (and the sign for Virgo is made a Christian symbol, after Raphael's Madonna). Clearly

30 Joshua Reynolds, *Captain Robert Orme* (1756)
. . . an officer under orders (see Plate 3)

Napoleon's charisma is neither secular nor simple. Though he had assumed the emergency powers of a Roman dictator when appointed First Consul, he did not give up those powers but added royal and divine offices. In fact, the differing outcomes of the two revolutions, American and French, can be put symbolically in the contrast between this picture of Napoleon I and Stuart's paintings of "George I" in all *his* regalia—namely, none: no epaulettes, orders, insignia. No wig, no sign of his office, no uniform, no presidential seal. Just the Citizen.

The secular and civilian ideal of Cincinnatus made American artists represent Washington, even in his military days, with great restraint. There was less emphasis on the glory of battle than on dutiful service. The city of Charleston rejected the painting it had commissioned from Trumbull, because it showed Washington standing by a theatrically rearing horse. Not for Washington the domination of "men on horseback" like Peter the Great as sculpted by Falconet or Napoleon as painted by David (Plate 2). When Thomas Sully attempted a heroic equestrian in his *Crossing of the Delaware,* it stayed rolled up in his studio, since he could not interest a buyer.

Trumbull spent hours sketching Washington at his riding exercises—Jefferson had described his fellow Virginian as the best horseman he had ever seen. But Trumbull used these sketches to show Washington as one officer among many at Trenton, at Princeton (Figure 29), at Yorktown (Figure 14). In this last painting, Washington is yielding the central position to General Benjamin Lincoln, who was allowed to accept the British sword of surrender, since he had been humiliated by the British when he surrendered Charleston to them.

The best painting of Washington with his horse is of the type shown in Joshua Reynolds' *Captain Robert Orme* (Figure 30). Orme, who became Washington's friend when they served together in the French and Indian War, is shown at his English estate; he has

31 Charles Willson Peale, *George Washington* (1772)
. . . orders shown, hands hidden

received his orders and is about to ride, responding to duty. (The convention of the soldier who has just been ordered to report was followed by Charles Willson Peale, in the first portrait ever done of Washington, in which the orders protrude from his pocket, Figure 31). In Trumbull's *General Washington at Verplanck's Point* (Plate 3), the horse nibbles at its own joint, as in Sir Joshua's painting (the device was famous from Van Dyck's portrait of Charles I; it lowered the horse's head below the human figure's). The pose is that of a man responding to his country's call. Washington's step-grandson said of this work: "The figure of Washington as delineated by Colonel Trumbull is the most perfect extant." He especially praised the stance, the large hands, the florid complexion. But what is even more interesting is the conception. We are given no ruler, no capering emperor or domineering conqueror, like Napoleon in the Alps. This is a citizen officer under orders. Cincinnatus.

PART TWO

THE FAREWELL

❦❦❦❦

OPINION

VI

NONALIGNMENT

> True fortitude is seen in great exploits
> That justice warrants, and that
>   wisdom guides,
> All else is tow'ring frenzy and distraction.
>   —Addison, *Cato* 2.1

ON A MONDAY morning, September 19, 1796, in the autumn of his second term as President, Washington left Philadelphia for his home in Virginia. Several hours later, Philadelphians opened *Claypoole's American Daily Advertizer* to read, on pages two and three, a lengthy article with the heading "To the PEOPLE of the UNITED STATES." Washington had given the editor his message, correcting proofs of it over the weekend, improving punctuation, "in which he was very minute." When the editor returned the autograph manuscript to Washington, he showed reluctance in handing it over, and Washington told him to keep it. It was valuable even before it was published.

One way to deepen his words' impact was to disappear before they could be read. He must place himself beyond any plea to reconsider. If his message was to be given full attention, he had told James Madison in 1792, the occasion of its delivery should not "be construed into a maneuver to be invited to remain" (Paltsits 14). He had rejected the idea of informing Congress of his decision while delivering the annual address to that body. In its formal

87

reply, Congress was bound to express regret at his withdrawal, and that "might entangle him in further explanations" (ibid. 11). A prolonged process of disengagement would blunt the force of his teaching. Washington foresaw (and forestalled) the kind of problem Lyndon Johnson faced in 1968, when he withdrew from the presidential campaign. The first President left no room for debate whether he really *meant* to resign. He presented the nation with a fait accompli.

To do so, he devised a novel form of communication, speaking not to the people's representatives in his normal way, but to the people themselves, with an immediacy that foreshadowed the "fireside chats" of radio and television days. Others quickly agreed to call Washington's message his "Farewell Address," but he gave it no more formal title than the republican salutation "Friends and Fellow Citizens." No doubt Washington would have hesitated to go "over the heads of Congress," with a direct appeal to the citizenry, if he were not resigning office at the same time. In the eighteenth century, such a procedure might be considered demagogic. But, for use this once, he liked Madison's suggestion that he speak to the people, "who are your only constituents" (ibid. 227), by way of the commercial networks of his time.

Washington released the authorized text to one newspaper, but he knew other papers would reprint it instantly. Three Philadelphia journals ran it later in the afternoon of *Claypoole*'s publication day. The day after that, in New York, the *Minerva and Mercantile Advertiser* could boast of its enterprise in getting the text to its readers. Some papers printed special editions or supplements containing the message. The *Courier,* in New Hampshire, alerted its buyers to the historic document they held in their hands: "We recommend to our customers a careful preservation of this week's paper, and a frequent perusal of its contents." (This paper first called the text a "farewell address.") That same day, two printers in Philadelphia brought out separate editions of the message in pamphlet form.

This was Washington's second great resignation, and he looked forward to it even more longingly than to his retirement from war. He had also given even more thought to the use of his departure as a didactic opportunity. The text would have to be carefully phrased, timed, correlated to his actions in urging the point home. In one sense, the message had not changed—a strong continental union expressive of "national character." But events, by 1796, had lent a special importance to that plea, in the light of Washington's embattled neutrality policy.

Even in 1792, when Washington had Madison draft (from dictated notes) the earliest form of the Farewell Address, he warned against sectionalism and division. This was the great danger to the vision Washington had for his country. He was as ardent a proponent of union as President Lincoln would be, and he had in some measure foreseen that this would be the great trial of the republic. At the end of the war he wrote: "I think the blood and treasure which has been spent in it has been lavished to little purpose, unless we can be better Cemented [a favorite term] . . . When the band of Union gets once broken, every thing ruinous to our future prospects is to be apprehended" (GW 27.50–51).

All the major political spokesmen of the day combined to dissuade Washington from resigning in 1792. But, by 1796, the sectionalism Washington feared had divided the country on the subject of Jay's Treaty. Washington drew up a number of new points for Hamilton to incorporate in the address. Washington would speak to Anglophiles and Francophiles alike, warning that "permanent, inveterate antipathies against particular Nations and passionate attachments for others should be excluded." He argued that American pledges to France, made during the Revolution, could not bind in perpetuity, since all foreign ties should be temporary & liable to be from time to time abandoned or varied, as experience and circumstances shall dictate; constantly keeping in view that 'tis folly in one nation to look for disinterested favors from another—that it must pay with a portion of its Independence for whatever it may accept under that character—that by such acceptance, it may place itself in the condition of having given equivalents for nominal favors and yet of being reproached with ingratitude for not giving more. There can be no greater error than to expect, or calculate upon real favors from Nation to Nation. 'Tis an illusion which experience must cure, which a just pride ought to discard (Paltsits 156).

Washington's opponents, in his second term, accused him of favoring England under the cover of neutrality. They could not see that the pressure of events was carrying America along with France, and Washington had to lean in the opposite direction to *arrive* at neutrality. The French were America's recent allies, and their revolution had, at the outset, proclaimed a legacy from Washington's own effort (as when Lafayette sent the key from the fallen Bastille to Mount Vernon). There were close personal ties between many Americans and political liberals in France. There was an ideological bond in the promotion of the rights of man.

England, by contrast, was the enemy so lately faced in arms; it still held to western posts; it fronted America with a long Canadian border, promising clashes; its monarch was leagued with others against the new doctrines of freedom. England's power on the sea was a constant menace to America's commerce. The logic of events should have carried America into wars that racked Europe in the eighteenth century's last decade. Washington was determined to prevent this, to form a peace with England, to oppose those who considered the French Revolution an extension of America's. He wanted America to follow its separate course, establish its unique ethos, free of any European system. Though he had won his fame in arms, he realized the nation should not fix its institutions in the midst of a military effort. Time must be gained for the country "to settle & mature its yet recent institutions" (Paltsits 158).

In retrospect, one cannot doubt the wisdom of Washington's policy. His lean toward England did not renew a love of monarchy in the people, partly because the only obvious candidate for that office found it so abhorrent (GW 24.272). And if that lean had not occurred, America could have been associated with the later excesses of the French Revolution, not only the Terror but the Empire. Jefferson, who also opposed association with any European system, was too optimistic that the French had swept away the old order and could be joined as part of a new world. The policies he advocated might have made America the ally of Napoleon, to Jefferson's own later horror. By the time of his own presidency, Jefferson was teaching the Washington doctrine on neutrality so emphatically that he gave it the catchphrase some still mistakenly attribute to Washington himself: "no entangling alliances."

Few realize how well educated Washington was in dealing with the foreign events of his day. He had served with the officers of both "superpowers" of his time. In 1754, he had triggered the opening engagement, near the Monongahela, of what became the first *world* war of the modern age, one waged from India through the Caribbean to the Mediterranean. France's loss of Canada in that war set up conditions favorable to America's Revolution, which nonetheless could not have been won unless France had reengaged the British in the West Indies. No one was more aware than Washington that his effort had been waged in the interstices of a larger, global struggle.

It should be remembered that Washington's first ambition was to serve, like his brother, in the British Navy. When he accompanied that brother to Barbados, he learned how a captain keeps his ship's log and kept such a record himself—a teenage glimpse of his aptitude for studying the conditions of command (*Diaries* 1.40–

71). Then, with his habits of observation, he had been a confidant of General Braddock and other British officers during the French and Indian War. By the time these men were on the other side— sometimes the very ones who had been involved in the earlier American war—he was coordinating his efforts with French officers who would take part in the early stages of their own Revolution. It embarrassed Washington that he could not retake coastal cities without the help of the French Navy; but he faced facts, and kept an army in the field for the day when, hurricane season having arrived in the Caribbean, he could finally persuade a French admiral to make a joint siege at Yorktown. To find his equivalent in the modern world, we would have to imagine the leader of some third-world "new nation" who had served with officers of *both* the Russian and the American military commands.

He knew both powers, and he would play one against the other; he feared absorption by either of them. He knew America's advantage came not from her own power but from the leverage given to a nonaligned force when the giants are locked in struggle for world domination. Only that course would give America the chance to establish its separate character, to defend the values it had proclaimed with such originality. Over and over, Washington said that America must be something set apart. As he put it to Patrick Henry, "In a word, I want an *American* character, that the powers of Europe may be convinced we act for *ourselves* and not for *others*" (GW 34.335).

This was a theme dear to Washington. He wrote to Timothy Pickering that the nation "must never forget that we are Americans; the remembrance of which will convince us we ought not to be French or English" (GW 35.154). A *national* character should be formed, one not bound down at home by narrow regionalism or tied to the fate of other nations abroad. As the Farewell Address put it, "The name of *American,* which belongs to you, in your national capacity, must always exalt the just pride of Patriotism" (Paltsits 142).

Washington had a better grasp of America's specific needs, prospects, and dangers than did any of his advisers, whom he consulted with great patience, trying to unite them around his neutrality. Despite claims that Washington was too dependent on Hamilton, Edmund Morgan has shown that Washington's policies of the 1790s were already formed in the 1770s. Washington had feared alliance with France, even while recognizing its necessity. He wanted no commitments that could be avoided. Even though his dear friend Lafayette suggested a joint American-French campaign to take Canada in 1778, Washington fought that suggestion with all his powers of persuasion. Openly, he sent a letter to Congress spelling out the military difficulties (Freeman calls this letter "one of the ablest that ever appeared over the signature of Washington," 5.85). Privately, he wrote Henry Laurens, president of the Congress, a letter he did not want the French allies, even Lafayette, to see. This letter Morgan calls "one of the more striking examples of the quick perception of political realities that lay behind Washington's understanding of power" (15). To return France to power in Canada would give that ally a purchase on this continent threatening to America's future. It would cement a union with the Indians that was already troubling to Washington. It would monopolize Newfoundland traffic. It would lead to a shift in the balance of power, giving France and Spain naval dominance. Such an alliance,

possessed of New Orleans on our Right, Canada on our left and seconded by the numerous tribes of Indians on our Rear from one extremity to the other, a people, so generally friendly to her and whom she knows so well how to conciliate; would, it is much to be apprehended have it in her power to give law to these states (GW 13.255–56).

Washington, so courteous to Chastellux and Rochambeau, so friendly with Lafayette, so dependent on d'Estaing and De Grasse, was determined not to auction off America's future. He was thinking far ahead. He knew that Louis XVI had not sent troops to America out of devotion to revolutionary principle. It served the King's interests to take advantage of England's distracting effort with her rebellious colonies. Interest was the only thing that made for proper relations between nations—and possession of Canada would give France different interests on this continent: "I fear this would be too great a temptation to be resisted by any power actuated by the common maxims of national policy."

Here, already, is the doctrine on treaties that we read in the Farewell Address. That doctrine was not inserted into the Address by Hamilton. Washington had penned it into his own first draft: "Nations as well as individuals, act for their own benefit, and not for the benefit of others, unless both interests happen to be assimilated (and when that is the case there requires no contract to bind them together)" (Paltsits 169). In the first draft, that became, as we have seen, " 'tis folly in one nation to look for disinterested favors from another." No member of his Cabinet prompted these views in Washington; in fact, no other could follow Washington's views in all their subtlety. Morgan concludes that:

his advisers never understood the operation of the policy as well as Washington did. Jefferson was bent on making a weapon of neutrality, on wringing concessions, especially from England, in return for American neutrality. Hamilton, on the other hand, was highly conciliatory in trying to restore commercial relations with England, and went almost past the limits of neutrality in his obsession with the ideological dangers presented by the French Revolution. Although Washington was closer to Hamilton than to Jefferson, neither of the two men fully grasped the sophistication of their chief's policy for the nation (23).

Washington was not carried away by French spokesmen—like Jefferson, who said of Genet in the early days of his mission, "He offers everything and asks nothing" (Freeman 7.75). Nor did the President share Hamilton's emotional revulsion from the French Revolution. He kept his head when very shrewd heads were spinning in odd ways.

Washington's policy had been wise when he expressed it in 1778, during plans for the Canadian campaign. It became even more relevant, though harder to maintain, after the execution of Louis XVI. That turned what had been a conventional war between superpowers into a worldwide ideological conflict of the sort we have been familiar with throughout the modern Cold War. We have experienced the baleful effects arising from the "permanent inveterate antipathies against particular Nations and passionate attachments for others." We have seen the world in terms of permanent blocs, where what is done by one part is taken as done by the whole. We entered Korea and Vietnam under the assumption that those countries were the instruments of China, and China of Russia. We delayed the split between Russia and China by denying that such a thing could occur. We welcomed the support of any nation so long as it was anti-Soviet, to the damage of our influence in the third world. We supported colonial powers if they were nonsocialist and opposed anti-colonial ones if they were socialist. We froze our responses by making them dependent on a single ideological test. What Russia was for we had to be against, and vice versa. Could there be a more complete fulfillment of the Farewell Address's warning?

The Nation, which indulges towards another an habitual hatred, or an habitual fondness, is in some degree a slave. It is a slave to its animosity or to its affection, either of which is sufficient to lead it astray from its duty and its interest (Paltsits 153).

What gave Washington his sensitivity to the power relationships between nations? The test and standard he constantly applied was that of "national character." He was still saying in the

Farewell Address what he had written as the war wound down thirteen years earlier: "We are a young Nation and have a character to establish" (GW 27.13). The most common use of "character" in the eighteenth century was as a synonym for "reputation," and the obvious parallel to Washington's concern with the national character was his care to protect his personal reputation, a care that has been criticized as excessive, if not obsessive. But he realized that a man's influence would be gauged by his credit in the broadest sense—not only his financial competence but the credibility of his word and the creditability of his actions.

Washington's strong support for Hamilton's financial program reflects a certitude that America would gain the respect from other countries so vital to self-respect only if it proved, from the outset, that it could "pay its way"—which meant, naturally, that it must also be willing to live within its means, in terms of power as well as of income. Washington had seen many talented Virginians lose control of their lives (and, often, possession of their plantations) as they let themselves slide into debilitating debt. It was the sad irony of Jefferson's later years that this opponent of the banks had to use them to juggle his increasing load of debts. Jefferson felt that agrarian virtue could be retained only if most men owned their own land; yet he was humiliated, in old age, by the need to ask for a public lottery to save Monticello. He was dependent on charity to save his estate for the last few years of his life, after which it went to his creditors.

The connection of credit with freedom is illustrated by the fact that Jefferson could not have freed his slaves, even if he wanted to. Virginia law made it mandatory to provide freed slaves with support, which made necessary a considerable fund that could be drawn on down the years. Washington, by careful management of his farms, was able to amass that fund for the freeing of his own slaves at Martha's death (Flexner 4.112–25, 432–48). As late as the 1830s, payments were still being made from that fund to Washington's aging freedmen. Jefferson's slaves, like his other possessions, were sold after his death.

Washington's vision of a nonaligned country making its own way in the world had the same roots as Jefferson's vision of the independent yeoman who retains the public virtue to be self-governing. As the nation should not become enmeshed in foreign systems of dependence, so the citizen should not be subject to this or that faction. Financial and intellectual independence go together. The freer one's actions, the more credit one will get for them, in ways that go far beyond economic accountability. Washington "purchased" trust in the war by refusing to let his services be purchased.

There is an interesting paradox—for the time, a fruitful one—in this conception of independence. It is what the followers of David Riesman would call an "other-directed" view of oneself. It depends on one's appearance in other people's eyes. After all, one does not give oneself credit—only creditors can do that. To have "character" was, etymologically, to bear a public stamp of approval, and the wider the public one submitted one's actions to for approval, the more the man of character had to *serve* that public, meet its expectations, solicit its good opinion. For many of Washington's contemporaries, everything turned on that crucial word "opinion."

VII

CHARACTER

> My life is grafted on the fate of Rome.
> —Addison, *Cato* 2.2

As CHARACTER, or reputation, rested on the opinion of others, so—David Hume argued—did government itself:

Nothing appears more surprizing to those, who consider human affairs with a philosophical eye, than the easiness with which the many are governed by the few; and the implicit submission, with which men resign their own sentiments and passions to those of their rulers. When we enquire by what means this wonder is effected, we shall find, that, as FORCE is always on the side of the governed, the governors have nothing to support them but opinion. It is therefore, on opinion only that government is founded ("Of the First Principles of Government," Green-Grose ed. 3.109).

It is the doctrine of James Madison in *The Federalist* No. 49:

If it be true that all governments rest on opinion, it is no less true that the strength of opinion in each individual, and its practical influence on his conduct, depend much on the number which he supposes to have entertained the same opinion (Cooke 340).

And of Rousseau:

What means has the government for shaping behavior? I respond: public opinion. If our conduct arises from our own feelings in solitude, it arises

99

from the opinion of others in society . . . Not reason, not virtue, not the laws can oversway public opinion unless one finds a means of changing the latter (*Lettre à M. d'Alembert,* Garnier ed. 176, 178).

In his later work *The Social Contract,* Rousseau was even more emphatic on the subject of opinion as the basis of all government:

To the three sorts of laws [mentioned] a fourth is added, more important than all the rest, one not inscribed in marble or bronze but in the hearts of citizens, which forms the state's real constitution; which daily acquires fresh power; which, while other laws become decrepit or extinct, reanimates or replaces them; which maintains a people in its institutional ethos and substitutes the force of habit for that of command. I speak of behavior, custom—above all, of opinion (2.12, Garnier ed. 272).

Like most ideas whose "time has come," this heightened regard for "opinion" drew together new and old insights that were already acting on the minds of the public. We can identify a number of these strands of influence:

1. The Scottish philosophy of moral sense gave a real or ideal spectator of human action an initiating as well as an evaluating role in moral conduct. Hutcheson and Hume said men were moved to benevolence by the sight of prior benevolences performed. Adam Smith made the "man within the breast" the audience to which one must play, the internalized "disinterested spectator." As we have seen, Gouverneur Morris praised Washington for exemplifying this moral code: "He beheld not only the affairs that were passing around, but those also in which he was personally engaged, with the coolness of an unconcerned spectator" (*Eulogies* 44). The man of public virtue solicits the good opinion of others, who become his imitators by virtue of their admiration.

2. A "spectatorial" social code was popularized by works like Lord Shaftesbury's *Characteristics* and Addison's *Spectator.* Self-improvement groups like those encouraged by Franklin in Philadelphia and Lord Kames in Edinburgh met to read aloud *Spectator*

CHARACTER

essays, to learn not only how to write but how to behave. A bourgeois code of civility was replacing, in political importance, the aristocrats' code of gentility. Washington was very much in the spirit of his age when, as a boy in his teens, he laboriously copied out rules of social conduct.

3. Montesquieu had won almost universal consent to his argument that no set of laws was workable unless it was tailored to the specific ethos (*esprit*) of the people to be governed. In Hume's terms, this meant that people would obey only where they had an opinion of right (these are the kinds of law they should obey) or of interest (obeying would repay them) or both. As John Adams wrote: "It is vain to expect or hope to carry on government against the universal bent and genius of the people" (*Works,* C. F. Adams ed. 4174–75). The same views led Hamilton, in *The Federalist* No. 84, to say that freedom of the press, "whatever fine declarations may be inserted in any constitution respecting it, must altogether depend on public opinion, and on the general spirit of the people and of the government" (Cooke 580). Madison agreed with him on this point: "The restrictions however strongly marked on paper will never be regarded when opposed to the decided sense of the public" (Jefferson *Papers* 14.20–21).

4. The cult of a legendary antiquity made men idealize small cities where the public business was conducted in the open and public virtue was maintained by a mutual surveillance of the citizenry. As Rousseau stated the ideal:

The ancients spent most of their life in open air, conducting their own affairs or attending to those of the state in public forum, walking in fields or gardens, or along the seashore, in rain or sun . . . Thus, in the glorious days of Rome, the citizens, keeping each other under constant scrutiny, were quick to accuse, from a zeal for justice (*Lettre à M. d'Alembert,* Garnier ed. 205, 209).

5. A corollary of this classical ideal was the encouragement of

philotimia in the good sense, a "love of distinction." If a citizen's conduct is always being put to the test, a desire to have that conduct vindicated is laudable. As Douglass Adair argued in *Fame and the Founding Fathers* and *The Spur of Fame,* love of glory was considered a virtue in the Enlightenment, which scorned the "monkish" ideal of hiding one's virtues or looking only to heaven for the recognition of virtuous deeds.

6. The "spectator" approach to moral motivation led to a rather crudely didactic philosophy of art, to a belief that one could instill virtue simply by depicting it. This made artists seek out heroes, to dramatize their virtue, to foster patriotism by allegorical display and public spectacles. Of course, a belief that art can have this effect, if sincerely held, will often *produce* the effect. As Hume says in his essay *Of National Characters:*

> The tenth legion of CAESAR, and the regiment of PICARDY in FRANCE were formed promiscuously from among the citizens; but having once entertained a notion, that they were the best troops in the service, this very opinion really made them such (Green-Grose 31255).

Such mutually enforcing concepts affected the way Washington was perceived—which, in turn, affected the way he acted. Within this context, it would be surprising, if not impossible, for a man of his importance not to show a deep concern for his "character," for the way he must look in other people's eyes. Alexander Hamilton expressed at times a rather kamikaze sense of honor, one that set the people at defiance: "It is long since I have learnt to hold popular opinion of no value" (*Papers* 17.366)—though even then Hamilton goes on to say he wants "the esteem of the deserving." Washington, by contrast, always wanted to engage the "opinion" of the public at large, as the only means of achieving solid political results. Not for him the grand if fruitless gesture.

In 1783, when he was pondering the best way to advise his countrymen on the need for a stronger union, he carefully con-

sidered the possibility that his effort might "backfire." Coming from
a military man, would it frighten the public as a sign of ambition
or of designs on civilian supremacy? As usual, he took soundings
in the opinion of others. To Hamilton he wrote:

My wish to see the Union of these States established upon liberal and permanent principles, and inclination to contribute my mite in pointing out
the defects of the present Constitution are equally great. All my private
letters have teemed with these Sentiments, and whenever this topic has
been the subject of conversation, I have endeavoured to diffuse and enforce them; but how far any further essay by me might be productive of
the wished for end, or appear to arrogate more than belongs to me,
depends so much upon popular opinions, and the timper and dispositions of People, that it is not easy to decide. I shall be obliged to you
however for the thoughts which you have promised me on this Subject,
and as soon as you can make it convenient (GW 26.276–77).

When, two months later, he decided to send his "legacy," he tried
to forestall the objections he feared by linking the statement with
his abandonment of any public office.

Washington was constantly testing public opinion and tailor-
ing his actions to suit it. If there was widespread fear that hereditary membership in the Society of the Cincinnati would create an
aristocracy, then Washington would abolish that item, though he
thought the public mistaken in its fears. Much as he wanted to
strengthen the union, he cautioned others not to move precipi-
tately in that direction until the public's sense of need had ma-
tured: "We are certainly in a delicate situation, but my fear is that
the people are not yet sufficiently *misled* to retract from error" (GW
28.431). Even when the drafting convention was called in Philadelphia, he refused to entertain very high hopes of the outcome; the
meeting could, in fact, hurt the cause it was meant to further if,
like the Annapolis convention, it should be ill attended (GW
29.198), or if the delegates should arrive too "fettered" by their
instructions to make major changes (ibid. 191–92). He feared, that
is, "a partial representation, or cramped powers" (ibid. 194). He

delayed his own decision to attend until these and other fears could be partly laid to rest by an active canvassing of opinion in several states. This constant attention to the mood of the people—to the receptivity, as it were, of his audience—deterred him from unrealistic projects, from grandiose schemes hatched more to satisfy his ego than to accomplish what was needed. He would have agreed with Shakespeare's Hotspur that it is senseless to call spirits from the vasty deep unless there is some prospect that, when you call them, they will come.

Washington realized that power is a tree that grows by a constant prudent trimming; that winning the people's long-term confidence is a more solid ground for achievement than either pandering to their whims or defying their expectations. This apparent paradox—that power grows by cutting it back—is far removed from the hydraulic view of power that fills so much of modern political writing, the view that power is drained away by so many vents and leaks that one should acquire the largest *amount* of it at every opportunity. Why, if you are carrying something in a sieve, pour out spoonfuls on your own? If, as General, Washington had accepted this latter view, he would have felt the ditherings of Congress so attritive that he must seize what powers he could as soon as he could. Instead, Washington felt that any immediate gain would be a loss in his primary assignment, to gain the trust of Congress so that it would give over a stable power in gradual increments—which is what happened. By not asking for too much, he finally got enough. We have all observed the kind of people who lose their hold on us by asserting it too soon, too massively, too possessively. Washington really did live by the maxim that one must win "the hearts of and minds of the people" (which is the fancy modern equivalent for Hume's "opinion").

This does not mean that Washington simply waited for the people to tell him what to do, then did it. The other side of his theatrical sense of audience was his feel for gesture, for just the right entry, or exit, or climactic move. By knowing his audience so well, he learned what would make them respond in useful ways—as when he shamed the officers into patriotism at Newburgh. And even there he was careful, in the theatrical interplay of confrontation and confidence, of rebuke framed as praise and bluff that looked like flattery, to address both the officers' "opinion of right" (what their honor obliged them to) and their "opinion of interest" (what they could do to strengthen his hand in pleading for them with Congress).

Public credit, once earned, must be put to use for the public good. The respect accorded him, to remain stable, must be grounded in the self-respect of his fellow soldiers, his fellow citizens. He tried to instill pride in his Army and prevent its humiliation, since—like Caesar's Tenth Legion—it would be formidable only if its opinion of itself was properly exalted. When Washington had formed his troops to hold their position at Harlem Heights, the British cavalry sounded, not the military recall, but a hunting call that the fox chase was over. As Joseph Reed remembered, "It seemed to crown our disgrace"—so Washington sent out his own men to make a demonstration of bravado while a larger force tried to encircle the foe. It was the first time in the war that the British were forced to flee (Freeman 4.198–201).

Washington showed a similar sense of occasion when he came upon the Pennsylvania militia dissolving into flight on the outskirts of Princeton. Personally rallying the troops, he shouted, "It's a fine fox chase, my boys," and again sent the British flying. The painter Charles Willson Peale and the sculptor William Rush were present with the Pennsylvania militia on that day, and later, when they compared impressions of the scene, Rush said of Washington:

I have been in battle immediately under his command—I have viewed him walking, standing, sitting—I have seen him at a game of ball, for several hours; exhibiting the most manly and graceful attitudes I ever saw. I have seen him dismount from his horse, a few hours after the Battle of Princeton . . . reviewing with great anxiety his little band, which had just taken the British 17th Regiment . . . At that moment of crisis . . . his likeness was worth more guineas than the British would have given for his person (Bantel 26).

As I mentioned earlier, Washington refused to accept Corn-wallis' sword from an underling, but directed Benjamin Lincoln to receive it—the man who had been denied the rites of war as he marched out of Charleston (Figure 14). When he asked the men whose term of service had ended to stay on so they could follow up the victory at Trenton, a subordinate began enrolling the volunteers who responded—till Washington said that men so generous could be trusted on their word (Freeman 4.333).

Washington's feel for the magnanimous gesture, which would not simply respond to opinion but summon it up, was repeatedly demonstrated. An important French ally, the Chevalier de Chas-tellux, was bound to him in a lasting relationship of respect and affection by this gesture at their first parting:

The weather being fair, on the 26th, I got on horseback after breakfasting with the General. He was so attentive as to give me the horse he rode on the day of my arrival, which I had greatly commended. I found him [the horse] as good as he is handsome, but above all perfectly well broke and well trained, having a good mouth, easy in hand, and stopping short in a gallop without bearing the bit. I mention these minute particulars be-cause it is the General himself who breaks all his own horses, and he is a very excellent and bold horseman, leaping the highest fences and going extremely quick without standing upon his stirrups, bearing on the bri-dle, or letting his horse run wild (Chinard 52).

Washington brought out the best in others, appealing to their sense of pride and duty. When he called out the militia to put down the Whiskey Insurrection, all five of his nephews were in the Virginia contingent. Before he left the troops at Fort Cumber-land, Washington called the oldest of them to him, and said he must set an example for his two brothers and two cousins. It was not an appeal anyone could treat lightly. In his last will, Washington left his swords to these five nephews, charging them

not to unsheath them for the purpose of shedding blood except it be for self-defence, or in the defence of their country and its rights, and in the latter case to keep them unsheathed, and prefer falling with them in their hands, to the relinquishment thereof (Freeman 7.589).

Washington could be as didactically effective with a yielding gesture as with an assertive one, as when—after the inauguration of John Adams—Jefferson motioned for the ex-President to precede him. Washington stepped back, indicating that he was simply a citizen again and would follow the new Vice-President (ibid. 437). At other times he used the majesty of his bearing to enforce discipline. When a delegate to the drafting convention of 1787 violated the members' pledge of secrecy by leaving his notes outside the chamber, Washington addressed the body in words reported by William Pierce of Georgia:

"Gentlemen, I am sorry to find that some one member of this body has been so neglectful of the secrets of the Convention as to drop in the State House a copy of their proceedings, which by accident was picked up and delivered to me this morning. I must entreat gentlemen to be more careful, lest our transactions get into the newspapers and disturb the public repose by premature speculations. I do not know whose paper it is, but there it is, let him who owns it take it." At the same time he bowed, picked up his hat and quitted the room with a dignity so severe that every person seemed alarmed; for my part I was extremely so, for putting my hand in my pocket I missed my copy of the same paper, but advancing up to the table my fears soon dissipated. I found it to be in the handwriting of another person. When I went to my lodging at the India Queen, I found my copy in a coat pocket which I had pulled off that morning. It is something remarkable that no person ever owned the paper (Farrand 3.86).

Washington clearly had the appearance, as Chesterton says in another context, of a great eagle walking with wings folded—and this, too, was a means of forming opinion.

VIII

FAME

Transplanting, one by one, into my life
His bright perfections, 'till I shine like him.
—Addison, *Cato* 1.5

HERO WORSHIP is a hard assignment for many people today—one they think they cannot fulfill, or should not. Hero worship is elitist. It reduces the science of history to mere biography, if not to anecdote. It suggests that individual talent is a more important force than large economic processes. Treating "the Fathers" as demigods encourages a childish attitude, or a belief in superior beings. The attitude of many in our time is captured by Bertolt Brecht's Galileo, who says: "Unhappy the land that needs a hero."

But it should be noted that the opposition to hero worship is itself elitist, since hero worship is a decidedly popular phenomenon, as civil rights workers in the South discovered when they saw pictures of Franklin Roosevelt and John Kennedy in poor black families' homes. Besides, the opponents of hero worship often show a lively devotion to intellectual heroes of their own, such as Marx. As I mentioned earlier, the revolutions that most proclaimed an impersonal historical process turned to the most personal of icons, a Stalin or a Mao, suggesting that hero worship may be, like "nature" in the Horace poem, impossible to dig out of people with any pitchfork.

Scientific history itself runs the danger of underestimating the mere element of chance, of randomness and muddle, in history—which often shows up in *personal* assertion or error. Clausewitz reminded his readers that the greatest commander can be undone by a subordinate, far off, who garbles his orders; a fact that can undercut one kind of "great man" theory, but one that makes personal activity—in this case, that of the subordinate—a crucial determinant of events. It was chance that took the tubercular Lawrence Washington to Barbados for convalescence, where the man's younger brother, accompanying him, caught a mild case of smallpox. Because of that train of accidents, General Washington was not vulnerable to the deadly waves of smallpox sweeping through his Army. An emphasis on the personal in history does not have to be part of any cult of great men in the Carlyle sense. It is often a recognition of the power of what Clausewitz called *Friktion,* of chance and the way it *uses* persons.

But there is no need to settle the balance between historical process and personal decision when we study the eighteenth century, since a belief in personal autonomy was part of the historical conditioning people underwent at that time. Large historical forces conspired to induce a belief in the possibility of human virtue and heroic achievement. Remnants of that belief perdured into the nineteenth century, which helps explain the great impact of Weems's *Washington* on young Abraham Lincoln. That belief was even more apparent when Weems was writing his book, with a certitude that the *description* of a hero could *produce* heroes among his readers. Could he have known of it ahead of time, he would have taken Lincoln's career as vindication of his theory.

It was also the theory of Thomas Jefferson, who set out systematically to create a pantheon of American heroes. He was active in commissioning the two greatest statues of Washington, Houdon's for Richmond (Plate 6) and Canova's for Raleigh (Figure 22). He fostered John Trumbull's plans for a series of popular engravings to celebrate the heroic acts of the revolutionary generation. Years later, his recommendation helped Trumbull, in his beleaguered old age, win congressional approval for the scheme to decorate the Rotunda of the Capitol with scenes of civic and military heroism.

Jefferson's principal contribution to the forming of a new heroic age was his fixing of the nation's architectural style as that of the Roman republic. His aim was expressly didactic, even propagandistic, and the extent of his devotion to his own program can be seen in his home, in the great house at Monticello. His very domestic arrangements were given a pedagogical pattern. Monticello's three public rooms are differentiated by the classical orders of architecture. The most formal room, the half-octagon parlor opening onto the garden, is done in motifs from Corinthian buildings, the most ornate order. Since its walls were mainly devoted to the fruits of European art and thought, Jefferson designed a special frame to hold pictures he had commissioned from Trumbull of his own three heroes, Bacon, Newton, and Locke, the "founders" of the Enlightenment.

The Ionic—the intermediate—order is used in the entry hall, with its emphasis on the natural sciences of the American continent. The ceiling relief of an American eagle presides over the room, around whose walls were specimens of American fauna, some brought back from the Lewis and Clark expedition. When Benjamin Latrobe's son visited the home during the period of the Greek revival, he was offended by the clutter and crowding of this early little museum of natural history. So many Indian artifacts were on display here that Jefferson called it his "Indian suite."

The lowliest order, the Doric, is saved for the dining room, with its depressed arches and simplest ornament. The room's walls had a special space for American scenes and architecture (including a print of Mount Vernon). The place of honor is the "tearoom" extension, a kind of secular apse, that held four "busts in plaister by Houdon": Washington and Franklin, the inevitable pair, along with Lafayette and John Paul Jones (Figure 32). Twenty-eight other American portraits were hung in tiers on the walls.

There is a puzzle here. Why did Jefferson reserve for America's political heroes the humblest of the three orders? He seems not only to put Washington and Franklin below European thinkers; he implicitly subordinates them to bison. Yet he called this room "my most honorable suite" (Letter of Feb. 7, 1820). The explanation is that rural virtue aspires downward, toward simplicity. Like Palladio, Jefferson associated the Doric order (the Tuscan variety of which he used on his home's final exterior) with Roman farms. In his earlier design for Monticello, the Doric ground floor was surmounted by an Ionic pediment at the second-story level, devoted to his library. After his return from France, he reduced that hierarchical exterior, which lifted scholarship away from the land, to the single order most expressive of rustic values. Though Jefferson distrusted members of the Society of the Cincinnati, he embraced the ideal of Cincinnatus, which is expressed in his shrine of republican heroes (where Washington appears in a painting as well as a bust, which means there were four representations of him in the house). The Enlightenment had its own uses for the idea that "the last shall be first." It is fitting for Jefferson's house to reach its paradoxical climax in the humble room devoted to serving the produce of the land. One entered his pantheon by way of a low door.

And, even more important, one arrived at it by a *classical* progression. Jefferson took the first steps that stamped America's fed-

32   Thomas Jefferson, *Tearoom at Monticello*
. . . secular apse, the heroes' shrine

eral city as a Roman town. In that sense, he prepared the site for
Washington's obelisk—just as he designed the secular temple at
Richmond that contains Houdon's statue. The republic of the
modern world aspired to be Roman in ways that amused the Irish
poet Thomas Moore during his visit while Jefferson was President:

> In fancy now beneath the twilight gloom,
> Come, let me lead thee o'er this second Rome,
> Where tribunes rule, where dusky Davi* bow,
> And what was Goose Creek once is Tiber now.

*Davus was the typical classical slave's name.

113

33   Louis-Léopold Boilly, *Houdon in His Studio* (1804)
. . . hero factory to the Enlightenment

This famed metropolis, where fancy sees
Squares in morasses, obelisks in trees,
Which second-sighted seers e'en now adorn
With shrines unbuilt and heroes yet unborn.

Jefferson took seriously what could only amuse Moore. The *philosophe* shied from the label of novelty as if it were an accusation. As Jean Starobinski put his attitude, "People did not want to innovate; they wanted to go back to forgotten origins" (104). The most radical imaginable break in history was, for the Enlightenment, an abrupt leap backward, over the medieval darkness, into antiquity's liberating air. New ideas were more daring the older they could claim to be. The great heroic models were literally *anti*-heroes, replacing the saints and priests of a preceding age. Men like Jefferson had a sense of moving deeper and deeper into the tunnel of time till they came out on the other side, where reason and freedom were at home under a Mediterranean sun. There was an oddly prescriptive note to their idea of freedom, as when Jefferson rebuked Benjamin Latrobe for offering his Capitol designs without a precedent, a warrant from Rome, the sort of authority Jefferson invoked for his cornices at Monticello.

But was Jefferson actually naïve enough to worship at his little republican shrine? Or was he just trying to manipulate others, create a myth of the republic that would awe the citizenry? His sincerity, it seems to me, is beyond doubt—he was certainly not "playacting" with Latrobe. But he *was* trying to manipulate others, as well. What seems to us naïve was, then, the newest doctrine on human conditioning and social management. Hero worship had a material base that made such "idealism" the coarsest realism. Virtue was no longer given from above, a grace from God. It was induced, here below, by contact—by "contagion," Hume said; by transmitted vibrations, according to Diderot; by sympathy, Adam

34   Giuseppe Ceracchi, *George Washington* (c. 1786)
. . . Jefferson's favorite image

Smith claimed; by a positive appetite for morality, triggered at the sight of benevolent acts, according to Francis Hutcheson. Human conduct was guidable by reason, according to the advanced thought of Jefferson's day; but reason itself told men to provide the material causes of benevolent activity. The eighteenth century aspired to make itself a hero factory; and in some measure it succeeded. Just look at Jefferson.

There was a literal "hero factory" in Paris, one that Jefferson frequented in his efforts to form a pattern of distinctively American heroism. This was the atelier of Jean-Antoine Houdon, shown in one of the paintings done of it by Louis Léopold Boilly (Figure 33). A little history of the Enlightenment could be written from perusal of this picture. Jefferson himself is on the shelf behind Houdon. We can single out the heroes of astronomy (Lalande), natural history (Buffon), music (Gluck), the theater (Sophie Arnould), law (Gerbier), the early revolution (Mirabeau), the *Encyclopédie* (Diderot and d'Alembert), and literature (Voltaire and Rousseau). Plutarch, by "ranking" the heroes (Greek and Roman) according to category, had suggested a taxonomy of the virtues — those proper to the warrior, the legislator, the orator, and so on. Here, on the shelf behind the seated Voltaire, Franklin and Washington appear in what had become, by the time of this picture (1804), a canonical pairing as the head and the heart of the American revolution.

Houdon's entire studio speaks of schooling in the antique. The live male model is paired with the cast of a female torso, under a classical relief and mask. The goddess Diana extends her right hand just above Houdon's modeling hand. The whole scene is presided over by Houdon's early Roman work, *The Flayed Man* (*l'Écorché*), partly modeled on the Doryphoros of Polykleitos; light streams in over the hand of that "fountainhead" work, combining the modern science of anatomy with ancient formulae. Voltaire, "echoing" (just above and to the left) the live model's seated posture, seems to wear a toga. Even Sophie Arnould, with one breast bared, is shown in her sacrifice scene from Gluck's *Iphigénie*.

On the top shelf over Voltaire's head (not distinguishable in this photograph), there are models for two full-length figures, one wearing sandals. John S. Hallam makes a persuasive case that these are clay studies Houdon made for the Richmond statue of Washington, models that Jefferson considered while advising Houdon on his countryman's portrayal. If this is the case, then Washington is a figure more extensively studied, in this picture of an artist among his works, than any historical figure except the seated Voltaire—an appropriate emphasis. Except for Voltaire, Washington is more prominent in the total *oeuvre* of Houdon than is any other person. Not only did the artist do the models, the many busts (often with subtle differentiations of character), the full-length statue; he also lobbied actively with Congress to create an equestrian Washington for the federal city.

A surprising aspect of Boilly's painting is the absence of Napoleon from the shelves (though Houdon had modeled Bonaparte at least two years earlier). Houdon was one of only two artists who did life studies of both Washington and Napoleon, each of whom (in his different way) seemed to resurrect the ideals of Rome. The other artist was Giuseppe Ceracchi, a revolutionary himself. Ceracchi traveled to America to create his Jovian likeness of Washington as President—Roman, with curls; not, perhaps, our image of the man (Figure 34). But some people, including Thomas Jefferson, thought it best captured Washington's majestic appearance. More to our taste, no doubt, is Houdon's portrait of Washington in retirement after the war—a Roman soldier, with tunic and sword belt (Figure 35). If one removes, in one's mind, the curls from Ceracchi's bust, the essential similarity of the portraits is apparent—the deep eye sockets, making the large nose even more prominent; the heavy eyelids; dead-level mouth; firm line of the jaw, but with a slight dewlap under the chin. Both severe. Both Roman.

35 Jean-Antoine Houdon, *George Washington* (c. 1786)
. . . soldier in his fifties

36   Maximilian Laboureur, after Giuseppe Ceracchi, *Napoleon* (c. 1802)
. . . gazing into the eternity of his renown

Ceracchi's life portrait of Napoleon has been lost; but the best copy seems to be by Laboureur, which shows a man gazing into the eternity of his own renown (Figure 36). Ceracchi's original may be lost because he became disillusioned with his old hero; plotted against him; and died on the guillotine in 1801. Houdon's best study of Napoleon, from 1806, wears a victor's fillet (Figure 37). Four classical busts, with subtle differences. How men interpreted Washington and Napoleon as reincarnations of the Roman

37   Jean-Antoine Houdon, *The Emperor Napoleon* (1806)
. . . the classical victor

would have a great deal to do with the histories of their respective countries.

The purpose of a hero factory like Houdon's was not simply to commemorate deeds already done but to call up virtuous actions in the future. As Starobinski says, the aim of the renewed Roman oath was "inventing a future" (104). Only when one's purpose was fixed, by examples from the past, could the future be shaped with a determination to impose new purpose. In a timeless

39 Titian Peale, *Interior of Peale's Museum* (1822)
. . . under the scrutiny of heroes

Rome, the will was forged to defy time, to bend its course. Houdon's busts, and those of other artists, were meant to carry Hume's "contagion" of public spirit. Great men were great by their communication with other heroes—as David Martin meant to tell us when he painted Franklin at work in the guiding presence of Newton (Figure 38).

America had its own "hero factory" in Charles Willson Peale's museum, which resembles in its program Jefferson's design for Monticello (Figure 39). European Science guides the whole, dividing nature into its Linnaean categories. Fauna are sorted and reduced to order along the lower tiers. Higher up are rows of portraits in which Peale honored the Revolution's heroes. On the right, busts modeled by William Rush are grouped in a neo-Plutarchan taxonomy (heroes of medicine, of politics, of war).

38   David Martin, *Benjamin Franklin* (1766)
    . . . Newton's heir under his gaze

The use of classical busts to define a new heroic age can be seen in Samuel F. B. Morse's portrait of Lafayette revisiting America (Figure 40). At the enshrinement of Voltaire in the Panthéon in 1791, men carried busts of the ancients (and of some moderns, including Franklin). The revival of Voltaire's *Brutus* in 1790 led to liturgical celebrations in which David's Roman bust of Brutus was enthroned on the stage. Mirabeau, present at a performance, was known to have adopted Brutus as his personal hero, and actors and audience connected specific lines with nods toward him. Later, when Mirabeau was painted by an anonymous artist, he was shown with the bust of Brutus.

The efficacy of such an explicitly didactic art was not doubted by an age that derived specific political events from performance of plays or exhibition of paintings. Alexander Pope said the aim of Addison's *Cato* was

> To make mankind in conscious virtue bold,
> Live o'er each scene, and be what they behold ("Prologue").

Timothy Dwight completed his epic *The Conquest of Canaan* "in order to raise the admiration, and inspire the love, of Virtue." Charles Willson Peale's fellow Pennsylvanians commissioned a portrait of Washington in order to promote virtue. In this spirit, plays by Voltaire and by Marie-Joseph de Chénier were given as integral parts of the French Revolution, and Addison's *Cato* was performed at Valley Forge during the ordeal of Washington's Army. At the 1790 revival of Voltaire's *Brutus,* the last scene was decorated and posed to reproduce the composition of David's painting *Lictors Returning Bodies of Brutus' Sons* (Figure 41); after the curtain, the actors came out and struck the pose of David's other "republican" picture, the *Oath of the Horatii* (Figure 12). Reporting on the evening, the *Chronique* wrote: "Never was illusion more complete; the spectators were as so many Romans; they all thought of themselves as taking part in the action."

40 Samuel F. B. Morse, *Lafayette's Visit to America*
. . . sunset on the republic's heroes

To shape one's behavior so literally after heroic models may seem artificial to us. But it was natural for men who thought Rome's greatness revealed the laws of nature and of nature's God. That explains Jefferson's slavish regard for Palladian proportions. Such "imitation" extended to the intimate details of one's life. Members of Princeton's Cliosophic Society took secret names, mainly classical, and were expected to live up to the ideals represented by their respective names. Joseph Warren wore (without ridicule) a toga into the pulpit when he delivered the Massacre Day oration in Boston; and then, after Warren fell at Bunker Hill, a youth at Princeton took the secret name of Warren—classical "playacting" had passed the ideal from antiquity to the present, and on into the future, in a line of living descent. One "caught" heroism from one's fellows, and spread the benign infection. As Plutarch, that patron of all hero worship, put it: "Nobility produces an impulse toward itself, and makes it a regular inclination" (*Pericles* 2).

To imitate live models from the secular pantheon was quite different from praying to dead saints. Jefferson said that, when he faced a difficult moral choice, he asked himself what Peyton Randolph would do in the circumstances—Randolph his admired cousin, the leader of the Virginia delegation to the Continental Congress. Or he asked what William Small, what George Wythe, would do—his teachers at Williamsburg. Life was a school for virtue, and one must find proper teachers. To a Diderot or Voltaire, Brecht's saying would make no sense at all. Does one pity the student who needs teachers?

Washington, as a teenager, copied out his rather wooden maxims on the proper bearing toward one's fellows, much as Franklin drew up his rigid training course in particular virtues. This last exercise has been praised or laughed at, treated as a worldly comedown from the Calvinist soul-searchings of Franklin's Boston forebears. But Franklin carefully dissociated his method

41   Jacques-Louis David, *Lictors Returning Bodies of Brutus' Sons* (1789)
        . . . outsuffering aristocrats

from theology in the very part of the *Autobiography* that introduced his plan. And though he prays for virtue, he does so with
the help of only one passage from Scripture (Solomon's praise of
wisdom), one passage from Cicero, and lines from James Thomson's poem beginning "Father of Light." The key motto, though,
is from that principal work of republican inspiration, Addison's
Cato. In that play of 1713, which was omnipresent in the revolutionary rhetoric of America, the aim is to "transplant" Cato's per-

fections into one's own life "till I shine like him." Cato's sons say they must

Copy out our father's bright example (1.1).

This worldly process, of heroic improvement of the will, was part of the Enlightenment project. Franklin's hero worship comes from Addison, not Calvin. It was of a piece with his reading *The Spectator* to form behavior.

To encourage the display of virtue, to make it more conspicuous, and therefore more contaminant, virtue should be conspicuously rewarded. And the only proper reward was *fame*. Fame should be freely sought and freely given. What Madison called, in *The Federalist* No. 10, "the most *attractive* merit" (Cooke 63) should be isolated for special celebration. Whence the cult of Washington. The purity of a perfect heroism was its willingness to be rewarded *only* in fame. This, for Benjamin Rush, was the whole difference between Washington and Napoleon: "The French and American Revolutions differed from each other in many things, but they were alike in one particular—the former gave all its power to a single man, the latter all its fame" (To John Adams, August 14, 1805). Even Hamilton could find common ground with his old foe Jefferson when it came to a judgment on Aaron Burr. He told others that Jefferson must be preferred to Burr because the latter desired power, not praise: "Mr. Burr has never appeared solicitous for fame, & that great Ambition unchecked by principle, or the love of Glory, is an unruly Tyrant who never can keep long in a course which good men will approve" (Hamilton *Papers* 25.323). Jefferson himself recommended Houdon to Washington as heroic in pursuit of the praise that comes from preserving the heroism of others: "I can assure you also that, as a man, he is disinterested, generous, candid and panting after glory, in every circumstance meriting your good opinion."

James Wilson, Madison's great ally at the Constitutional Convention, taught his law students that virtue was born from fame, and preserved by it:

The love of honest and well earned fame is deeply rooted in honest and susceptible minds. Can there be a stronger incentive to the operations of this passion, than the hope of becoming the object of well founded and distinguishing applause? Can there be a more complete gratification of this passion, than the satisfaction of knowing that this applause is given—that it is given upon the most honourable principles, and acquired by the most honourable pursuits? (*Works,* McCloskey ed. 405).

The love of reputation and the fear of dishonour are, by the all-gracious Author of our existence, implanted in our breasts, for purposes the most beneficent and wise. Let not these principles be deemed the growth of dispositions only which are weak or vain; they flourish most luxuriantly in minds, the strongest and, let me add, the most humble (ibid. 593).

Fame was thus a social glue, a structural element, for the republic in its early days—not only for Washington, but for all those called to service. Charles Royster has acutely analyzed the indissolubility of heroic acts and their reward (207):

An officer summarized much of his concern for his reputation in the word "honor." The term referred not simply to his own conscience or self-esteem, but also to public acknowledgement of his claim to respect. To have honor and to be honored were very close, if not the same.

Here we come to the very nub of our problem with the hero. Madison said that it was crucial for the success of the experiment in an *extended* republic that it choose representatives of "the most diffusive character" (most *extended* reputation) as well as "the most attractive merit." Hero worship was not just an adjunct to this program, an epiphenomenon, adventitious. It was, for a while at least, at the center of the whole endeavor. If we cannot grasp that, we shall miss one large aspect of the revolutionary process.

I have been speaking of hero worship, not simply of heroism. I suppose that humankind can always use heroes; but the social demand for them differs from age to age. And rarely was the demand more important than in the Enlightenment, in the first and most successful revolution inspired by that age's ideals. Washington did not create the republic. The republic created him. It called for him, asked him to live up to its expectations. Royster, again, puts the matter justly (260):

Americans often talked about the kind of inspiring leader they wanted. In practice, they did not want a powerful commander at all—that is, a man to whom they would delegate coercive authority. Rather, they wanted someone whose eloquence or example could make them want to do what they knew they ought to do. The reluctance with which Americans went to war, in contrast to the enthusiasm with which they demanded independence, made such a figure very important to the success of the revolution.

Washington was asked to be heroic, but heroically restrained. Not only did he (and he alone) play a crucial role at *every* stage of the revolution—in the war, the postwar period, the passage of the Constitution, and the establishment of a working government. He had to show a complete virtue, a complementarity of competing traits, that was asked of no other. There may have been greater warriors than he—but Arnold proved venal, Gates petty, Charles Lee unstable. Others might *use* armies better; but Washington best grasped that the problem was to *create* an army, to keep it in existence, by embodying its cause. There were better philosophers of the republican ideal. But the assurance of Washington's example swayed more people than did their arguments. Jefferson and Hamilton offered brilliant analyses of events, in the first administration; but Washington steered a steadier course than either could. He did not come to describe heroism, but to enact it. As Alexander Pope put it in the introductory verses to Addison's play, Washington showed men the difference between "What godlike Plato *thought* and Cato *was.*" Washington's disinterested service, in war and peace, in power and in retirement, was not flawless; but it was so rounded and balanced that, for people with a less classical ideal of rule, it looks *soporifically* perfect. We actually prefer our great men to have flaws. The doomed greatness of a Caesar or Cromwell or Napoleon seems to crash against the limits of the world, to batter Lucretius' *flammantia moenia mundi,* suggesting by failure what still might be achieved. But people of Washington's time loved limit; they did not want to break out of this world, which was a new place for them, recently won back from heaven; where they were content to dwell, if someone could show them how. Washington embodied the classical ideal of restraint described by Addison:

> True fortitude is seen in great exploits
> That justice warrants and that wisdom guides.
> All else is tow'ring frenzy and distraction (*Cato* 2.1).

An effort at recovering those classical emphases will, strange to say, expose one to the charge of romanticizing. People, we will be told, do not really act from noble dreams. In Washington's time, as in ours, interests jostled, conflicts occurred—of classes, of regions, of race. Of course. That is the common element in human history. But even the way one justifies selfishness reflects what *does* change from era to era, the ideals various people feel drawn to. The acceptance of a norm makes a difference even to one's *departure* from that norm. And it certainly makes a difference to whatever chances there are for human nobility in the scuffle and strivings of history. As Malraux said, a nation must be judged by the statues it puts up.

I should make it clear that I do not describe the ideal expressed in the cult of Washington because I think it the highest ideal, or one appropriate for any other time. In many ways, our own ideals are superior to those of the revolutionary period— more egalitarian, certainly; and in some ways more compassionate. That does not mean that we live up to our ideals, any more than other ages have. But the possibility for heroism in our time will be tempered by the ideals we propose to ourselves—a thing proved in the heroic age of civil rights, when Dr. King and many others suffered and died for the concept of equality we profess but have not lived up to. Gilbert Chesterton said that Lincoln did not go to war to express his opposition to slavery; but, when the opportunity arose, he could issue the Emancipation Proclamation because his views were formed, just waiting their chance. In that sense, says Chesterton, the heaven of abstraction can at times send lightnings down.

The secular ideology of the revived republic had its own limits. That is not surprising. Neither are failures to live up to it. The surprising thing is how often men did respond as they claimed they should. The hero factories did, after all, produce some heroes. Was it accidental to Warren's heroism at Bunker Hill that he had assumed the toga, in fact as well as in his mind? The most famous sayings of Patrick Henry and Nathan Hale bear a suspicious resemblance to verses in Addison's play; which makes some doubt that they were spoken. But the important thing is that people would *assume* they had been said, would *expect* such things—which may mean that the expectation was understood by Henry and Hale as well as by their audiences. Jefferson looked to the most powerful man in his society, Peyton Randolph of the mid-seventies, as a moral exemplar—which means the society was doing some of the things it aspired to. Should we, with Brecht, pity those in need of Cato? Jefferson would pity those deprived of him.

IX

ROLE

Behold young Juba, the Numidian Prince,
With how much care he forms himself to glory.
—Addison, *Cato* 1.1

YOUNG STUDENTS at Princeton took ancient names to identify themselves with the ideals under their study. George Washington, who never learned Latin (or any foreign language) acquired his sense of ancient ideals from more popular channels, principally the theater. The cult of antiquity was not, in the eighteenth century, confined to the learned; it could be disseminated in the popular works of which Mason Weems's are a late but powerful example— and through means other than books. Even among the learned of that time, classicism was less a matter of accurate scholarship than of political mythmaking. All but a few knew their ancient history, much as medieval believers knew their biblical history, through ritual and icons and theater. What the ordinary person might know about Cincinnatus, in the Enlightenment, was no doubt as sketchy (but numinous) as what the ordinary person of earlier times knew about St. Paul.

Even the learned were, as we have seen, naïve by our standards, in the belief that they could reenact the past, assume the ancient heroes' names and qualities. In this respect, Madison's contemporaries at Princeton were no different from George Wash-

133

ington reflecting on his favorite play, Addison's *Cato*. It was a play he knew intimately, one he cited often. He plays constant variations on his two favorite lines:

> And shows thee in the fairest point of light (1.2).

> In the calm lights of mild philosophy (1.1).

He also cites the play's most famous lines:

> 'Tis not in mortals to command success,
> But we'll do more, Sempronius, we'll deserve it (1.2).

At the age of twenty-six, going back toward battles in which he had seen so many die, he identified himself with the Numidian prince who yearns for a prize he cannot have, Cato's daughter. He wrote to Sally Fairfax, the wife of his best friend: "I should think my time more agreeable spent believe me, in playing a part in Cato, with the Company you mention, and myself doubly happy in being the Juba to such a Marcia, as you make" (GW 2.293).

Earlier, Washington had written to Sally that he went back to the frontier only for "my own Honour and country's welfare" (ibid. 287). Juba is the character in *Cato* most concerned with honor; it fills his speeches and those of other characters describing him.

> Better to die ten thousand thousand deaths
> Than wound my honour (1.4).

> Honour's a sacred tie, the law of Kings,
> The noble mind's distinguishing perfection,
> That aids and strengthens virtue, where it meets her,
> And imitates her actions, where she is not (2.5).

Men were quick to quote such verse at a time when the lines between "real life" and art were made deliberately fuzzy. Indeed, later memories of people like Nathan Hale and Patrick Henry were intertwined with echoes of the play:

> What pity is it
> That we can die but once to serve our country (4.4).
>
> Gods, can a Roman Senate long debate
> Which of the two to chuse, slavery or death? (2.1).
>
> If we should sacrifice our lives to honour,
> Or wear them out in servitude and chains (ibid.).
>
> To sue for chains . . . (ibid.).
>
> It is not now a time to talk of aught
> But chains or conquest, liberty or death (2.4).

Though Washington could identify himself with Juba in his youth, the play's obvious moral paradigm is its title character. Even within the play, characters urge each other to pattern themselves on Cato's example:

> I'll hasten to my troops,
> And fire their languid souls with Cato's virtue (1.5).

In Voltaire's *Mort de César,* Cassius emboldens Brutus with these words (3.3):

> *Caton forma tes moeurs, Caton seul est ton père,*
> *Tu lui dois ta vertu, ton âme est tout à lui.*

And Brutus responds:

> *À mânes de Caton, soutenez ma vertu.*

Although Washington clearly adopted the values of this play, it would no doubt be stretching things to look for specific instances of his imitation of Cato. Forrest McDonald has made the attractive suggestion that Cato putting down the conspiracy of Sempronius in Act III, scene 5, was a model for Washington's defeat of mutiny at Newburgh. But nothing could less resemble the courteous skill of Washington, in that difficult situation, than Cato's harsh reproaches ("Hence, worthless men!"). A closer parallel might be drawn between Cato's actions and the rebuke Washington gave to delegates from the western Pennsylvania counties engaged in the Whiskey Insurrection—but even there Washington used tact and persuasion so far as possible. Not only did he address the militia sent west as "my fellow citizens in arms" (GW 34.6); he insisted that they remain "scrupulously regardful of the rights of their fellow citizens" (Flexner 4.175) in the resisting counties. As always, he insisted on civilian supremacy, telling Henry Lee, the commander in chief, to

aid and support the civil Magistrate in bringing offenders to justice. The dispensation of this justice belongs to the civil Magistrate and let it ever be our pride and our glory to leave the sacred deposit there unviolated (GW 34.6).

The formative influence of Addison's play is probably to be sought less in any positive model it gave Washington than in what it warned against in verse after verse: Caesarism. Cato is praised in Plutarch as the great opponent of Caesar's rise, just as Brutus is praised for accomplishing his fall. The contrast between Cato and Caesar was recognized as paradigmatic even by their contemporaries—as we can tell from the fact that works (now lost) were written on that contrast by Cicero, Brutus, Hirtius, and by Caesar himself. Fortunately, Lucan's epic on the same theme is extant. Playing Caesar and Cato off against each other was a regular method of arguing moral points, as when Richard Steele contrasted the severity of virtue with the easygoingness of corruption:

Caesar's bounty, munificence, popular and sumptuous entertainments, stole an universal affection; Cato's parsimony, integrity, austere and rigid behavior commanded as universal reverence. None could do an ungentle thing before Caesar, none a loose one before Cato. To one 'twas recommendation enough to be miserable, to the other to be good. To Caesar all faults were pardonable, to Cato none. One gave, obliged, pitied and succored indifferently; the other blamed, opposed, and condemned impartially. Ceasar was the refuge of the unhappy, Cato the bane of the wicked. Cato had rather *be* than *seem* good; Caesar was careless of either, but as it served his interests. Cato's sword was the sword of justice, Caesar's that of ambition. Caesar had an excellent common sense, and right judgment of occasion, time, and place; the other blunt man understood no application, knew how to be right, but was generally so out of season. Caesar's manner made even his vice charming, Cato's even his virtue disagreeable. Caesar insinuated ill. Cato obtruded good (*Christian Hero* 15–16).

Caesar was the very archetype of tyrannical success, as Cato was of noble failure. In Lucan's words:

> *Victrix causa deis placuit, sed*
> *Victa Catoni (Pharsalia* 1.128).
>
> Gods favor conquerors, Cato the conquered.

Addison puts the same theme this way:

> Dost thou love watchings, abstinence, and toil,
> Laborious virtues all? Learn them from Cato;
> Success and fortune must thou learn from Caesar (2.4).

> What is a Roman that is Caesar's foe?
> Greater than Caesar, he's the friend of virtue (2.2).

Addison's play, the most popular one in eighteenth-century America, taught Washington and many others to fear the ambitions of a Caesar. Even to be accused of admiring Caesar was an insult in America, as we can see from a famous anecdote. Jefferson, in an 1811 letter to Benjamin Rush, described how he had received Hamilton, his fellow cabinet member, at his home in Philadelphia. The year was 1791:

The room being hung around with a collection of the portraits of remarkable men, among them those of Bacon, Newton and Locke, Hamilton asked me who they were. I told him they were my trinity of the three greatest men the world had ever produced, naming them. He paused some time. "The greatest man," he said, "that ever lived was Julius Caesar."

At one time, this view of Hamilton fit with his apparent use of the pseudonym "Caesar" during the ratification debates. But Jacob Cooke has cleared Hamilton of authorship in this instance. (WMQ 1960). And Thomas Govan has established that, with only one exception (a neutral reference to Caesar's skill), *all* Hamilton's written references to Caesar are condemnatory (WMQ 1975). Hamilton regularly said that a republic must fear "a Caesar or a Cromwell," its "Catilines and its Caesars." He described Burr as an aspiring Caesar. In fact, he once compared Jefferson's protestations of modesty to "Caesar coyly refusing the proffered diadem." Jefferson clearly misrepresented Hamilton's view of Caesar.

I earlier argued that rejection of the Moses image was important in the development of Washington's cult—it showed that a classical and secular heroism was desired, not a theological one. It is just as important that Washington was never compared with Caesar, was always contrasted with him—considered his equal, at the least, in stature, but his superior in virtue. I have found only one image of Washington that gives him the appearance of Caesar's bust; and it is clearly based on a misunderstanding of Canova's statue. A European engraving in the McAlpin Collection of the New York Public Library shows Washington, in a seated position, writing the Constitution (Figure 42). He is "Caesar giving the laws." But the pose is taken from Canova's Raleigh statue (Figure 22), which was known in Europe from prints and models; and Canova presented Washington as a dutiful soldier resigning. The print maker has mistaken the Farewell Address ("Amici e Concittadini") for the Constitution.

Nothing in Washington's actions suggested the ambition of a Caesar, and there is no American memorial in that guise. If he had been tempted in that direction, the Society of the Cincinnati would

42 Anonymous, *George Washington Giving the Laws*
. . . Canova misconstrued

have given him the ideal instrument for his use. Formed by Henry Knox, its membership was composed of officers serving at the end of the Revolution, or those who had served for three years at officer level, and their direct male descendants. The Society was attacked by those who feared it would form the basis of a military aristocracy. Hugh Henry Brackenridge, Madison's classmate at Princeton, mocked the society in his 1786 Hudibrastics. He said the first Cincinnatus returned to his plow

> Without a goose-resembling bauble
> Or other bird or beast could gabble
> A word of Latin or Greek (*Cincinnatus* 17).

Actually, Benjamin Franklin had rightly questioned the Latin the bird gabbled (*Omnia Relinquit Servare Rempublicam*). But, even with his misgivings, Franklin knew how to get on both sides of any issue: he joked about the Society, then accepted honorary membership in it.

Brackenridge makes noncommissioned soldiers grumble in rhyme:

> Because we have not at our bosum
> That thing of yours, a rosy cruzum;
> Are not embellish'd with a broach
> At heart, or neck, or breast, or crotch.

The Connecticut Wits, themselves Cincinnati, counterattacked in verse. David Humphreys mocked Aedanus Burke, who pamphleteered against the Society:

> Scar'd at the shape of Cincinnatus'name,
> The envious Burke denied that road to fame,
> Stars, ribbands, mantles crowding on his brain (*Anarchiad* Bk. 7).

Critics of the Society saw that its real power would come

from its association with Washington, and they tried to drive a wedge between him and it. When Mirabeau's pamphlet appeared in a 1786 translation, it said of Washington:

Was it possible he should not feel how much his name was superior to all distinctions? The hero of the Revolution which broke the chains of half the world—was it possible that he should not scorn the guilty, dangerous, and vulgar honor of being the head of a party?

Jefferson, too, wrote Washington from the Congress sitting in Annapolis:

I have wished to see you stand on ground separated from it; and that the character [reputation] which will be handed to future ages at the head of our revolution may in no instance be compromitted in subordinate altercations . . . [since] the moderation and virtue of a single character has probably prevented this revolution from being closed as most others have been by a subversion of that liberty it was intended to establish (Jefferson *Papers* 7.105–6).

Washington had asked Jefferson for his objections to the Society, in preparation for his own attendance at the first general meeting. This had the effect of all Washington's requests that critics put their objections in writing—Jefferson tried to make his animus less evident, his criticisms seem as moderate as possible; so that Washington had him on record as saying: "I have no suspicion that they [the Society's founders] foresaw, much less intended those mischeifs which exist perhaps in the forebodings of politicians only" (ibid. 105). But Jefferson went on to criticize the honorary memberships (which "might draw into the order all the men of talents, of office and wealth"), the hereditary feature (which might "procure an engraftment into the government"), and the national meetings (which might lead to public controversy). Washington not only took these objections to heart, but went to Annapolis to confer with Jefferson before attending the Society's meeting in Philadelphia.

At that meeting, Washington moved for all the reforms Jefferson had suggested, and threatened to resign the office of president of the Society, just conferred on him, if the meeting did not endorse his motion. Washington's own notes on these reforms paraphrase Jefferson when they do not directly quote him:

Strike out every word, sentence, and clause which has a political tendency. Discontinue the hereditary part in all its connexions, *absolutely,* without any substitution which can be construed into concealment, or a change of ground *only;* for this would, in my opinion, encrease, rather than allay suspicions. Admit no more honorary Members into the Society . . . Abolish the General Meetings altogether (GW 27.393–95).

Washington also asked, though not as one of his nonnegotiable demands, that the members "discontinue the order" (stop wearing the eagle emblem designed by Pierre l'Enfant) lest people suspect it "is a feather we cannot consent to pluck from ourselves, tho' we have taken it from our descendants" (ibid. 396). Washington himself never wore the eagle from this time on, though the French officers sent him one encrusted with diamonds and emeralds. Officer after officer from the revolutionary times had his portrait painted (by Charles Willson Peale and others) wearing the eagle on its blue ribbon — Peale even showed his brother James wearing it in the privacy of his studio. John Trumbull had the eagle sculptured onto his own portrait bust (Figure 43), and the statues of French officers in Lafayette Park, across from the White House, wear the sculptured order. But Washington did not allow himself to be represented wearing that or any other order. (Members of the Cincinnati later had it *added* to prints taken from paintings by Edward Savage and Gilbert Stuart.)

When the officers at the Philadelphia meeting opposed Washington's reform plan, which amounted — they saw — to a virtual annihilation of the body, he brought his formidable will to bear upon them. Nothing short of the *unanimous* abolition of the he-

43   Robert Ball Hughes, *John Trumbull* (1834)
. . . eagled in perpetuum

reditary feature in all state branches would induce him to remain in the Society (not to mention his remaining president):

General Washington arose, and again opposed this part as particularly obnoxious to the people. In a very long speech, and with much warmth and agitation, he expressed himself on all the Parts of the Institution deemed exceptionable, and reiterated his determination to vacate his place in the Society, if it could not be accommodated to the feeling and pleasure of the several States (Winthrop Sargent, "Journal of the General Meeting").

It was Newburgh all over again—officers banded together to defy civilian "opinion," and only Washington able to quell them. We know how important this matter was to Washington from the fact that he revealed his emotions in public, and made a long speech, things he normally tried to avoid. He was using again his old instrument, the creative power of surrendering, a threat to resign. The Society would be disgraced from its inception if he refused to join it. What would the "Cincinnati" be without Cincinnatus himself? The general meeting adopted his proposals.

After that meeting, some state societies denied that their representatives could bind them. Three states refused to ratify the reforms. Two years later, Massachusetts, which had adopted them, reversed itself. Washington, meanwhile, limited his presidential activities to the minimum of signing membership forms for foreign officers who applied. He was planning to resign his presidency before the next national meeting (1787) and was keeping open the threat to resign membership if the Society engaged in politics. He was in a "delicate situation" again, able to restrain his officers by the bonds he hoped to maintain with them, refusing to wear the order or encourage enthusiasm about the Society, firmly steering them away from politics by his threat to resign, yet constantly aware that his "character" was at stake if the Society should cause division in the union he was trying to foster. He had surrendered his own power in order to promote that union. He thought the Society should do the same; but he must try to make it a voluntary surrender, not a crushing condemnation of a whole body of men, an act that would itself divide the community and drive much talent and good will outside the common effort.

Washington has been criticized for attacking, during his presidency, the "democratic societies" which had ties with the early French revolutionaries, while he remained president of the Cincinnati, with their foreign officers as members. Some of these critics do not look at the obverse of this argument, that Jefferson, who had warned against the Cincinnati for their foreign connection, welcomed the aid of the democratic societies. But the record shows that Washington retained his membership in the Society only to check it—and that he succeeded. None of the fears entertained of it were confirmed by events. He did not use his presidency of the nation to enhance the glory of the Society. Washington's sincerity in this matter is seen from the way he moved to block the formation of "patriotic societies" working for his *own* favorite cause of a stronger government in 1786. When his nephew Bushrod Washington wrote enthusiastically about the formation of such societies, Washington opposed the plan:

Generally speaking, I have seen as much evil as good result from such Societies as you describe the Constitution of yours to be; they are a kind of imperium in imperio, and as often clog as facilitate public measures . . . May not a few members of this society (more sagacious and designing than the rest) direct the measures of it to private views of their own? (GW 29.22).

Washington clearly had the Cincinnati in mind as he tried to prevent this accession of "allies" to their presumed cause. In correspondence with members, he had deplored the failure of some states to ratify his reforms (GW 28.350). He told them that public fears had been allayed, but only by the reforms; and the fears were likely to flare up again if there was further retreat from the reforms (ibid. 240). In 1785 he wrote to Hamilton:

The fears of the people are not yet removed, they only sleep, and a very little matter will set them afloat again. Had it not been for the predicament we stood in with respect to the foreign Officers, and the charitable part of the Institution I should, on that occasion [the Philadelphia meeting], as far as my voice would have gone have endeavoured to convince the narrow minded part of our Countrymen that the Amor Pate. [Patriae] was much stronger in our breasts than theirs, and that our conduct through the whole of the business was actuated by nobler and more generous sentiments than were apprehended, by abolishing the Society at once (ibid. 352).

Washington's coolness toward the Society was signaled when he affected not to know what was going on in state branches except his own (which had fully endorsed his reforms). Then, in the fall of 1786, almost a year before the next national meeting, Washington sent another of his circular letters of resignation, this one to the state societies, announcing that he could not attend the next meeting because of private business and telling them, "It is my desire not to be reelected to the Presidency, since I should find myself under the necessity of declining the acceptance of it" (GW 29.31). He expressed, in the letter, approval of the Society as "now constituted" (i.e., by the reforms adopted at the last meeting). To Henry Knox, the "father" of the organization, he expressed the misgivings this action was meant to indicate:

Are not the subsidence of the Jealousies [suspicions] of it, to be ascribed to the modification which took place at the last Genl. Meeting? Are not these rejected in toto by some of the State Societies, and partially acceded to by others? Has any State so far overcome its prejudices as to grant a Charter? Will the modifications and alterations be insisted on, or given up, in the next Meeting? If the first, will it not occasion warmth and divisions? If the latter, and I should remain at the head of this order, in what light would my signature appear in contradictory recommendations? In what light would the versatility [changeableness] appear to the

Foreign members, who perhaps are acting agreeably to the recommendations of the last General Meeting? (ibid. 194).

These were, in effect, Washington's instructions to Henry Knox
on what would be needed to guarantee that Washington did not
withdraw from membership as well as the presidency. He confided
his strategy to Madison:

I might be charged with dereliction to the Officers, who had nobly supported me with uncommon marks of attention and attachment. On the
other, with supporting a measure incompatible (some say) with republican principles. I thought it best therefore without assigning this (the
principal reason) to decline the Presidency, and to excuse my attendance
at the meeting on the ground, which is firm and just; the necessity of
paying attention to my private concerns . . . Professing at the same time
my entire approbation of the institution as altered, and the pleasure I feel
at the subsidence of those Jealousies which yielded to the change. *Pre-
suming,* on the general adoption of them (ibid. 114–15).

Washington was deftly letting it be known that anyone shopping
around for an American Caesar need not apply at Mount Vernon.
More than that, he was letting it be known that he would oppose
anyone who might aspire to that role.

But the letter to Madison was prompted by a consideration
that would complicate Washington's sense of his own role, and
lead to considerable agonizing. Madison had informed him of the
effort to hold an amending convention in Philadelphia in the late
spring of 1787. Madison argued that Washington's presence at that
meeting was crucial; but that was just the time when the Cincinnati would be holding their general assembly. Aside, even, from
Washington's pledge not to reenter public life, this circumstance
forbade his going to the city after he had told the officers that his
private affairs would not allow him to travel:

I should think it incompatible with that candour which ought to char-
acterize an honest mind, not to declare that under my present view of

the matter, I should be too much embarrassed by the meetings of these two bodies in the same place, in the same moment (after what I have written) to be easy in the situation; and consequently, that it wd. be improper to let my appointment stand in the way of another (ibid. 115).

He repeated the same thing to Governor Edmund Randolph, when that official begged him to join the Virginia delegation (ibid. 198). A delicate situation had become, apparently, a tragic one. Washington's conception of duty, of his obligation to forswear even the appearance of Caesarism, was depriving him of any opportunity to help his country achieve the union for which he had fought. For months he wrestled with this insoluble problem, testing other men's opinion, refusing a place in the delegation, asking almost hopefully if the effort at Philadelphia was not doomed anyway. Because, if it was not, his sense of his own role might need to be recast.

PART THREE

THE CONSTITUTION

❰❰❰ ❰❰❰ ❰❰❰ ❰❰❰

FOUNDER

X

LAWGIVER

His virtue renders our assembly awful.
—Addison, *Cato* 1.2.

ON MARCH 28, 1787, four months after he had turned down Madison's request that he attend the Philadelphia convention, Washington agreed to go, in a letter to Governor Edmund Randolph that was full of ifs and hedges:

However, as my friends, with a degree of sollicitude which is unusual, seem to wish for my attendance on this occasion, I have come to a resolution to go, *if* my health will permit, *provided,* from the lapse of time between the date of your excellency's letter and this reply, the Executive may not, the reverse of which wd. be highly pleasing to me, have turned its thoughts to some other character; for independantly of all other considerations, I have, of late been so much afflicted with a rheumatic complaint in my shoulder that at times I am hardly able to raise my hand to my head, or turn myself in bed. This, consequently, *might* prevent my attendance, and eventually a representation of the State; which wd. afflict me more sensibly than the disorder that occasioned it. *If* after the expression of these sentiments, the Executive *should* consider me as one of the Delegates, I would thank your Excellency for the earliest advice of it; because, *if* I am able, and *should* go to Philadelpa., I shall have some previous arrangements to make (GW 29.187, italics added).

Washington twists and turns so restlessly, trying to keep open his avenues of escape, that he tangles his grammar, saying the *reverse*

of which would please him, rather than what he clearly means—
which would please him.

This letter has exasperated some readers. Even so devout a
Washingtonian as Douglas Southall Freeman called it "an equivo-
cal, overcautious and self-regarding letter" (Freeman 6.83). Freeman, indeed, finds that Washington's correspondence through this
whole period shows "an amazingly egocentric strain" and a "pa-
tent regard for himself, as distinquished from his country" (ibid.
84). Freeman's hero had, for once, let himself become "too much
the self-conscious national hero and too little the daring patriot"
(ibid. 86). That is a strong indictment, coming as it does from
one who studied Washington so closely and so well.

What Freeman cannot forgive is that, even as late as the end
of March, less than two months before the scheduled meeting,
Washington "took superlative pains not to commit himself beyond
easy withdrawal" (ibid. 83). But, given the sad failure of attendance at the earlier two conventions, in Alexandria and Annapolis,
Washington had good reason to fear that this one, too, would be
ill attended or crippled by the delegates' instructions. By expressing his fear of this outcome, in so many directions, Washington
spurred on the effort to prevent such a failure. That was understood by his correspondents, who asked that his name appear pro-
visionally on the list of Virginia delegates. On the one hand, it
might convince others that this convention would be a serious
gathering—as David Humphreys said: "If you were determined
to attend the convention, and it should be generally known, it
would induce the eastern states to send delegates" (Marshall 5.108).
On the other hand, if the project should fizzle, Washington's name
could be removed from the list. Madison assured him: "A sus-
pence of your ultimate determination would be no wise inconve-
nient in a public view, as the Executive [of the state of Virginia]
are authorized to fill vacancies and can fill them at any time"
(Madison *Papers* 9.224). Washington's name, as he knew very well,

was being used as a bargaining chip to up the ante in Philadelphia: "The advantage of having your name in the front of the appointment as a mark of the earnestness of Virginia, and an invitation to the most select characters from every part of the Confederacy, ought at all events to be made use of" (ibid. 199). Thus the "hesitations" Freeman attacked were a conscious stratagem, one approved of by the very people urging him to attend.

Even so, one state (Rhode Island) did not send a delegation, and that from another state (New York) withdrew; and the instructions to the delegates were so binding that the convention went into secret session to defy them. It was risky enough for Washington to break his pledge against further participation in public life; to spend his moral capital on an empty scheme would have made him look not only inconsistent but foolish.

No one, it turned out, invoked against Washington his earlier renunciation of public office; but Washington refused to treat that as lightly as others did. What Freeman calls an undue regard for his own reputation was, for Washington, a point of honor, a matter of keeping his word. He was being asked, it might be, to exchange the "character" of a Cincinnatus for that of a turncoat. As he wrote to Governor Randolph:

I declare to you that my assent is given contrary to my judgment, because the act will, I apprehend, be considered as inconsistent with my public declaration delivered in a solemn manner at an interesting [crucial] area of my life, never more to intermeddle in public matters. This declaration not only stands on the files of Congress, but is I believe registered in almost all the Gazettes and magazines that are published (GW 29.198).

Freeman wonders what would have happened if the public had known, at the time, "all the disparaging circumstances of Washington's hesitation" (6.86). But it was essential to the Cincinnatus role, as that was understood by Washington's contemporaries, that he should not only feel a reluctance to taking up power of any sort, but express that reluctance. One reason Washington made his assent provisional was to determine whether respectable public opinion held him, still, to that promise. If it had, Washington would have been forced to withdraw. He could hardly lend credit to the effort in Philadelphia if his very doing so *dis*credited him.

His friends argued, naturally, that Cincinnatus had as great a duty to leave his plow at this time of national peril as he had done the *first* time; and Washington admitted that this argument from duty was the strongest one. He feared that his refusal to attend would be "considered as dereliction to [desertion from, cf. GW 29.114] republicanism" (ibid. 171). If, in some way, the risking of his "character" could do the country good, he was bound even to that sacrifice.

But what if, as a result of the Philadelphia meeting, he could be accused not merely of inconsistency or self-seeking, but of trying to *hurt* his country, of overthrowing its government? The deepest level of Washington's concern is rarely discussed. More than most men, he showed an early and unblinking awareness that the Philadelphia convention would engage in acts not only "irregular" or extralegal, but very likely illegal. John Jay had alerted him to this problem as early as January. Jay—whom Washington would appoint his first Chief Justice, for his legal acumen—thought the Annapolis convention's call for a new meeting in Philadelphia was unconstitutional. Only in retrospect, to distinguish it from the document that replaced it, do we refer to the constitution in force in 1786 as "the Articles." For men of the time, it was *the* Constitution: and that Constitution prescribed only one way of amending—by initiative of *Congress,* ratified by *all* thirteen states. The Annapolis convention initiated a call to the states (bypassing Congress), even though only four states were legally represented in Annapolis. The states began responding, appointing delegates, without waiting for Congress to act—six would elect delegates before Congress belatedly issued its own call, on February 21.

Jay thought that, if conventions were to be held (themselves not provided for in the Constitution), Congress would have to issue a new call for them in each of the states, with a national convention to be formed only by delegates from these.

> To me the policy [prudence] of such a convention [as called for at Annapolis] appears questionable; their [the delegates'] authority is to be derived from acts of the State legislatures. Are the State legislatures authorized, either by themselves or others, to alter constitutions? I think not (*Corr. and Papers,* ed. Johnston, 3.228).

John Marshall, a successor to Jay as Chief Justice, also grasped the legal point when he studied Washington's correspondence:

> By many, a convention not originating in a recommendation of congress, was deemed an illegitimate meeting . . . There were many who discountenanced the convention, because the mode of calling it was deemed irregular, and some objected to it, because it was not so constituted as to give authority to the plan which would be devised (Marshall 5.105, 110).

Washington, too, understood the legal obstacles—but he saw further than Jay did. Even if Congress should join the effort, somewhere down the line, that would not make the process any more legal under the prevailing constitution. At most it would lend a "colouring," open to endless legal challenges. He wrote to Jay on March 10 (before he learned that Congress had just issued its call):

> In strict propriety a Convention so holden may not be legal. Congress, however, may give it a colouring by recommendation, which would fit it more to the taste without proceeding to a definition [establishment] of the powers. This however constitutionally it might be done would not, in my opinion, be expedient: for delicacy [misgivings] on the one hand, and Jealousy [suspicion] on the other, would produce a mere nihil (GW 29.177).

Constitutional conventions had been the instruments of the revolutionary governments in 1776; and Washington now thought, in the wake of Shays's rebellion, that advocates of change should take the most direct route to placing a new plan before the people, without a nice regard for procedures that were bound to be broken, as indeed they were. (Washington could not know, at this time, that the convention's delegates would agree to hide their first illegal steps by pledging themselves to secrecy.) He had already written to Henry Knox on February 3, shortly after getting Jay's letter:

The legallity of this Convention I do not mean to discuss, nor how problematical the issue of it may be. That powers are wanting, none can deny. Through what medium they are to be derived, will, like other matters, engage public attention. That which takes the shortest course to obtain them will, in my opinion, under present circumstances, be found best. Otherwise, like a house on fire, whilst the most regular mode of extinguishing it is contended for, the building is reduced to ashes. My opinion of the energetic wants of the federal government are well known; publicly and privately I have declared it; and however constitutionally it may be for Congress to point out the defects of the foederal System, I am strongly inclined to believe that it would not be found the most efficatious channel for the recommendation, more especially the alterations, to flow, for reasons too obvious to enumerate (ibid. 152–53).

During the very time when Washington is accused of dithering, he was realistically testing the chances of success for a scheme that, in order to succeed, would have to defy the Constitution in force, ask men to break their oaths to it, and overthrow the government in place. As a general, Washington had learned to count the cost of possible failure before launching an attack. In this major gamble of his life, no one had more to lose than he, and no one was more honest with himself about the probable stakes of a meeting in Philadelphia.

It was clear, for one thing, that Rhode Island, already in virtual secession even from the government in place, would not agree to any stronger scheme—which meant that the convention would have to defy the constitutional provision for unanimous agreement to any change. Once that step was taken, any "coloring" of legality for the process of change would disappear. At some point, Wash-

ington surely learned—what he must have suspected anyway—
that Madison planned to arrive in Philadelphia with a plan that
moved the adoption of a new government to be adopted by state
conventions, *not* the legislatures. Once that motion was taken up,
every delegate would be at odds with his instructions to amend
within the guidelines of the Articles. And if that step were made
known to the public, the delegates would be so busy defending
their first steps that they would be able to take no others; the
debate would be less among themselves than with their foes in
public, at home in their state legislatures, or in the federal Congress. All the procedural fights that did follow on the eventual
publication of the draft would have been conducted simultaneously with the debates on further changes to be made. So the
pledge of secrecy was made, and enforced by Washington; and the
embarrassing record of the convention's procedures was entrusted,
at the final session, to Washington, who took it to Mount Vernon,
where few would dare to challenge him for its surrender. (As has
often been noted, if that record had come to light at the time of
the ratification debates, the Constitution would never have passed.
Madison's original plan, with a stronger central government able
to veto state laws, and a stronger veto on congressional legislation,
would have confirmed the worst fears of the antifederalists.)

For us, the "Constitutional Convention" (not known by that
title at the time) is bathed in a rosy glow of ultimate vindication.
Its outcome looks inevitable. But for many it was what William
Findley called it, the "dark conclave." Samuel Bryan, writing as
"Centinel" in one of the most widely reprinted attacks on the new
scheme, characterized the draft this way:

The evil genius of darkness presided at its birth; it came forth under the
veil of mystery, its true features being carefully concealed, and every de-
ceptive art has been and is practising to have this spurious brat received
as the genuine offspring of heaven-born liberty (Storing, *The Complete
Anti-Federalist* 2.164).

There would have been many more such denunciations but for the sacred names of Franklin and Washington, linked to the fate of the draft. Even with that immeasurable advantage, passage of the new constitution was a very close-run affair. Without the "great names," it is unlikely the plan could have succeeded. But Washington had to be aware, from the outset, of the other side to this calculation—that, should the proposal fail, his name would be connected with an effort to subvert the government, to make its officers abandon their oath that union under the Articles would be perpetual.

Even at the convention, delegates had to face, over and over, the gravity of what they were suggesting. When McHenry of Maryland said this plan asked his countrymen to break their oaths of office, Madison airily answered that it was asking this of *all* the states:

The difficulty in Maryland was no greater than in other States, where no mode of change was pointed out by the Constitution, and all officers were under oath to support it. The people were in fact, the fountain of all power, and by resorting to them, all difficulties were got over. They could alter constitutions as they pleased (Farrand 2.476).

Later, writing as a New Yorker named Publius, Madison made the same defense of the convention's conduct:

They [the delegates] must have reflected, that in all great changes of established governments, forms ought to give way to substance; that a rigid adherence in such cases to the former, would render nominal and nugatory, the transcendent and precious right of the people to 'abolish or alter their governments as to them shall seem most likely to effect their safety and happiness' (*The Federalist* No. 40, Cooke 265).

By quoting the Declaration of Independence, Madison granted the *revolutionary* nature of the changes proposed. A whole new government had been submitted to the people, to be addressed by state conventions popularly elected. If they accepted the plan, it would go into effect. If not, then the suggestions of the drafting convention were simply (as Madison put it) "some *informal and unauthorised propositions,* made by some patriotic and respectable citizen or number of citizens" (ibid.).

Madison's words call for a careful reading, because they both formulate a classic problem of government and echo a famous solution to that problem. If the people are to have the opportunity to change their government, then some one or some group "unauthorised" (since their act *precedes* the consent of the people) must have the audacity or effrontery to suggest that change. Rousseau had put the matter this way:

The people who submit to laws should institute them; since those bound together by the law can alone set the conditions of this bond. But how are they to set them? By joint impulse, or sudden inspiration? (*Contrat* 2.6 Garnier ed. 259).

His answer is that a legislator must *propose* the laws he has no power to *pass.*

He holds no office, and does not partake of the sovereign. His task, which is to institute the republic, has no place within that republic's constitution (2.7, 261).

He who frames laws has no power, and should have none, to pass laws. The people cannot, if they would, rid themselves of this inalienable power (ibid. 262).

Now look again at Madison's argument:

. . . the transcendent and precious right of the people (cf. Rousseau's *droit législatif . . . droit incommunicable*) to 'abolish or alter their governments as to them shall seem most likely to effect their safety and happiness' (cf. *il n'appartient qu'à ceux qui s'associent de régler les conditions de la société*); since it is impossible for the people spontaneously (*par une inspiration subite*) and universally (*d'un commun accord*), to move in concert towards their object; and it is therefore essential, that such changes be instituted (*qui constitue la république*) by some *informal and unauthorised*

propositions (ce n'est point magistrature, ce n'est point souveraineté), made by some patriotic and respectable citizen or number of citizens.

Since Madison's library perished in the University of Virginia fire of 1895, and he drew up no catalogue of it, there is no way to establish whether he owned or had read *The Social Contract* by 1787. But wherever he got his argument, the drafting convention of 1787 was a perfect fulfillment of Rousseau's concept of the lawgiver. It was a body irregular and powerless, outside both the constitution it replaced and the one it proposed; it defined its own role and then disappeared. Whatever guilt was incurred in defying the sanctioned government, the convention took that guilt with it into oblivion. If it was wrong to speak for a new government before the people had authorized this, such speaking became the necessary *condition* for the people's speaking. Thus Machiavelli had spoken of the legislator as a scapegoat, taking on himself any crimes or violations necessary to radical change (*Discourses* 1.9) —the role Shakespeare assigns to his Henry IV:

> God knows, my son,
> By what by-paths and indirect crookt ways
> I met this crown, and I myself know well
> How troublesome it sate upon my head:
> To thee it shall descend with better quiet,
> Better opinion, better confirmation;
> For all the soil of the achievement goes
> With me into the earth (H. IV II, 4.5).

Rousseau has a more positive vision of the legislator as surrendering personal power in order to animate the laws: "When Lycurgus legislated for his country, his first act was to give up the throne" (*Contrat* 2.7, Garnier ed. 261). This ideal of surrendering power to establish it is obviously close to the role Washington had forged for himself. Although the convention as a body is the literal fulfillment of Rousseau's concept, Washington is the personal embodiment of it. True, he would assume power later, un-

44   Hyacinthe Rigaud, *Bossuet, Bishop of Meaux*
. . . in the arsenal of learning

der a different title, after the convention had gone out of existence. But he was the palladium, the protective symbol, of the
convention—a role the Federalists played up and the anti-Feder-
alists had to find some tactful way of minimizing. And his preeminence was not, as we often hear, because he was a "war hero."
People did not admire a conquering Caesar in him, but a Cincinnatus resigning. He embodied the ideal of limited power, restrained and checked, but with a dignified authority. He could
symbolize this because he had served without pay; he had surrendered his own commission; he had checked the 1783 mutiny at
Newburgh and in Congress; he had repressed the Pennsylvania
mutiny; he had reformed and controlled the Cincinnati; he had
retired from public life for four years, despite the urgings of many
people that he take a hand in federal or state government; he had
yielded with manifest reluctance, and only after many requests, to
serve in the convention. By all these acts, he confirmed the image
that made him trustworthy to the citizenry, as he had been to
Congress during the war. When one thinks of the surrender of
power, one's mind goes more easily to him than to the convention. Rousseau almost seems to be describing him when he frames
the task of the *législateur:*

For a people just coming into being to favor sound views of government
and act on the basic rules of political necessity, effect would have to
become [its own] cause; the social affections, which their institutions are
supposed to shape, would have to foster them; men would have to be,
without the laws, what the laws would have them become. That is why
the legislator shall not use either force or [mere] argument. He must
resort to another kind of authority entirely, an ability to lead without
compelling and persuade without proving (*Contrat* 2.7, Garnier ed. 262).

I asked earlier how Washington was able to understand the
strategy of gaining power by yielding it; and one answer lay in the
dictatorial ideal of Cincinnatus and Fabius, solving the problem of
succession to a charismatic leader by building the promised surren-

45 William Rush, *George Washington* (1815)
. . . modern philosopher

der into his very charisma. Popular "opinion" asked of Washington what he was prepared to give it. But there is a further kind of leadership, based on archetypal roles, that transcends even the charismatic leadership of men in crisis. This mythical form of leadership is timeless and institutional, not merely temporary and personal. It lifts the people into a sphere "larger than life" by its expression of an abiding myth.

The Queen of England is mythical even when she is not charismatic. She may be both—but the myth is stable, an office; the charisma is volatile, a quality. The office does not depend on day-to-day revalidation by the proofs of "grace." So, Pope Paul VI was mythical but not charismatic. Pope John Paul II, for a time at least, was both. Charisma is ad hoc—bred out of, and addressed to, crisis; born of instability, and often perpetuating it. Myth is perduring; it weaves a continuity between the generations. The mythical office tends to be inherited; the charismatic quality is instantaneous.

Washington was a charismatic leader in time of war. But his peaceful role as founder was mythical. This seems to pose a paradox, since he did not inherit his offices—in the Cincinnati, at the convention, as President—but inaugurated them. Yet the myth of the founder *is* a paradox. It puts *inaugurators* in a *tradition;* and, even more important for Washington's sense of power, the classical tradition of founders made them give power to the law by divesting themselves of it in person.

Bacon had taught his followers that the highest form of human greatness belonged to *conditores imperii,* and especially to the founders of republics, those men glorified by Machiavelli (*Discourses* 1.10). Plutarch's omnipresent *Lives* began with a string of founders carefully balanced and compared. And the recurring note among the greatest founders is their self-abnegation in the very act of bringing law to the state. Plutarch said of Theseus, "Surrendering the kingship as he had promised, he gave order to the com-

46 Francesco Lazzarini, *Benjamin Franklin* (1791)
. . . ancient philosopher

47 Joshua Reynolds, *Lady Stanhope as "Contemplation"*
. . . bluestocking at daybreak

monwealth" (24). Lycurgus, widely held to be the greatest lawgiver, began his task with an abdication (3) and ended it with suicide, lest the state depend more on his person than his laws (29). For the same reason, Solon left Athens after his legislation was in place (25). And when Romulus was unwilling to leave Rome, the gods took him away for the state's good (28).

Washington in his deepest role, as founder, as father of his country, lived up to this classical pattern. He was not seen as a lawgiver in the autocratic sense, Caesar or Moses issuing the divine orders he alone could communicate (cf. Figure 42). The representation of him as a wise man of the law follows the "philosopher in his cabinet" type, a type made familiar by portraits like Hyacinthe Rigaud's *Bossuet* (Figure 44)—the sacred orator is shown surrounded by his arsenal of learning, prepared to preach what he has learned by deep study. When William Rush was asked to sculpture Washington as President, he made him this kind of philosopher, with books and column and scroll (Figure 45)—echoing the treatment of Franklin by Lazzarini (Figure 46).

The suppleness of this tradition is demonstrated in Joshua Reynolds' brilliant variation on it, *Lady Stanhope as "Contemplation"* (Figure 47). This bluestocking is portrayed at the end of a long night of study and sketching. She had braided her hair, put on gown and slippers, then worked alone till sunrise—we see it behind her. Her gown falls like the toga in Polyeuktos' "philosophical" pose for Demosthenes. (The eighteenth century restored the lost hands of Demosthenes with a scroll in the left one, instead of joining them.) Demosthenes stands before his audience, preparing to speak, like Bishop Bossuet:

> As when of old som Orator renound
> In *Athens* or free *Rome*, where Eloquence
> Flourished, since mute, to som great cause addresst,
> Stood in himself collected, while each part,
> Motion, each act won audience ere the tongue . . . (*Paradise Lost* 9.670–74).

The philosopher holding his scroll was painted by Thomas Sully for West Point, which wanted a picture of its seventy-eight-year-old founder, Thomas Jefferson (Figure 48). The effect of a toga is given again by the robe. The figure has a poise that has outlasted vigor; a glow fuzzes the sunken features, like the flare of an expiring memory. All power has gone out from the man into the pillar of the republic, against which the sharply defined edges of the Declaration are lit. It is a moment of vulnerable triumph, which melted James Fenimore Cooper's hostility toward Jefferson:

You know my antipathies, as you please to call them, to Mr. Jefferson. I was brought up in that school where his image seldom appeared, unless it was clad in red breeches, and where it was always associated with the idea of infidelity and political heresy. Consequently I would have gone twice as far to see the picture of almost any other man. The moment I entered the library and cast my eyes on the picture, I desired the gentleman with me to wait . . . There was a dignity, a repose, I will go further and say a loveliness, about the painting that I never have seen in any other portrait . . . I saw nothing but Jefferson, standing before me, not in red breeches and slovenly attire, but a gentleman, appearing in all republican simplicity, with a grace and ease on the canvas, that to me seemed unrivalled. It has really shaken my opinion of Jefferson as a man, if not as a politician; and when his image occurs to me now, it is in the simple robes of Sully . . . (*Letters* 1.95, 1823).

Since this is the only life-size life-portrait of Jefferson, Rudulph Evans used it as the model for his statue in the Jefferson Memorial (Figure 49); but he stuck Rembrandt Peale's fifty-seven-year-old head on Sully's seventy-eight-year-old body. While the body shifts back to rest, the head stares forward in defiance. The shoulders, caught between, make a stiff effort at negotiating this odd conjunction. The result is neither oratory nor resignation, but mere stubbornness of planted feet.

Perhaps the most famous political use of the "philosopher in his study" theme is David's 1810–12 portrait of Napoleon (Plate 4). Like Lady Stanhope, Napoleon has been hard at work all night— the candle has burnt down; the clock stands at 4:13 A.M. He rises

48   Thomas Sully, *Thomas Jefferson* (1821)
     . . . the pillar's strength is the document's

SWORN U

WE HOLD THESE TRUTHS TO BE SELF-
EVIDENT: THAT ALL MEN ARE CREATED
EQUAL, THAT THEY ARE ENDOWED BY THEIR
CREATOR WITH CERTAIN INALIENABLE
RIGHTS, AMONG THESE ARE LIFE, LIBERTY
AND THE PURSUIT OF HAPPINESS, THAT
TO SECURE THESE RIGHTS GOVERNMENTS
ARE INSTITUTED AMONG MEN. WE···
SOLEMNLY PUBLISH AND DECLARE, THAT
THESE COLONIES ARE AND OF RIGHT
OUGHT TO BE FREE AND INDEPENDENT
STATES···AND FOR THE SUPPORT OF THIS
DECLARATION, WITH A FIRM RELIANCE
ON THE PROTECTION OF DIVINE
PROVIDENCE, WE MUTUALLY PLEDGE
OUR LIVES, OUR FORTUNES AND OUR
SACRED HONOUR.

to stretch and relax; puts his hand in his waistcoat. (The gesture, common in eighteenth-century paintings of men at ease, is the equivalent of putting one's hands in modern pants pockets.) He has earned his moment of rest, having just completed, all by himself, the *Code Civile*. He has seal in hand to authorize this final draft. But it is a civil code written by a military man; he may have put his sword aside while he wrote, but his uniform is still on, decorations and all. He has not worked with a prior body of law to bind him. The book on the floor, next to some designs by David himself, is a Plutarch, expressing the idea of personal heroism involved in this labor; for Napoleon works in godlike isolation, a type of the romantic individual creating new worlds from his head in a splendid loneliness. If he has not brought down the tablets from Sinai, one feels, he has smuggled them out of the Castle of Otranto. His imperial chair has not only the royal orb and bees, but the thunderbolt of Zeus. Napoleon told David, "You were right to show me working while my people sleep."

My people—it has a different ring from Canova's *Amici e concittadini*, "fellow citizens." The contrast helps us grasp Stuart's vision of Washington as political philosopher (Plate 5). Washington, too, has risen from his writing desk; but he steps forward with a gesture of greeting for a visitor. It is not an oratorical gesture like that of the Prima Porta Augustus, but one taken from conversation pieces (see Praz Nos. 61, 64, 105, 106, 136, 142, 155, 156, 214, 242, 258). The regalia of office are here—the column of order, the drapes of court, the seat of authority, the opening onto vistas of power. Yet Washington's chair gives the literal basis of his authority—thirteen stars for the states, woven together with the binding yet bending ribbons of federal connection. The rainbow of the new political covenant circles that chair, not the temporary holder of it. There are books under the working table here—as in Rigaud's Bossuet, Reynolds' Lady Stanhope, David's Napoleon. Two of the three books give the history of Washington's military

49   Rudulph Evans, *Thomas Jefferson* (1943)
       . . . Rembrandt Peale's head on Thomas Sully's body

career—his General Orders and a history of the American Revolution. They are history now, since Washington wears no uniform or decorations. The third book is the Constitution, marking the limits of his power. On the table, where Washington has been attending to official correspondence, are the signs of law binding him, the *Federalist* and the *Journal of Congress*. He sits here to execute the will of others, not to impose his own. The stylized eagle and fasces on table and chair are not personal emblems, but national. Washington greets others because he is not alone; he is part of a process, a government by discussion with others. As political philosopher, he engages in a dialogue, not a lone act of creation. Others will sit in his chair and do what he has done. The same authority will be wielded, the same limits observed.

Stuart put his Athenaeum portrait on a body modeled from a man shorter than Washington, and of a very different build. The figure is woodenly posed, even more awkward than Evans' statue. Yet, in this ambitious Lansdowne portrait, the man who rarely did backgrounds or settings with any care, just sketching them when he did not leave them out or turn them over to an assistant, has devoted special skill to rendering the attributes of office in this picture—which *are* the attributes of the office, not of the man. This third type of Stuart portrait does not, as some have claimed, belie the simplicity of his other two. Here, as well, the emphasis is on *Citizen* Washington, the founder giving men laws by giving up power.

XI

SACRIFICE

> His sufferings shine, and spread a glory round him.
> —Addison's *Cato* 1.1.

JUST AS HE had feared, Washington was accused, by enemies of the newly drafted Constitution, of lending his name to a conspiracy against government. Since the accusers had to be cautious in their treatment of two such great names, he and Franklin were normally called dupes of the plotters, rather than coconspirators. But that "excuse" applied more obviously to Franklin, who might be too old to know what he was doing, and was certainly too old to exercise any power under the new arrangement. Washington, by contrast, was more vigorous—and correspondingly more to blame. Samuel Bryan called him the Trojan Horse inside which the whole false scheme could be hidden and then smuggled into the republic:

This horse was introduced by their hostile enemy the Grecians, by a prostitution of the sacred rites of their religion; in like manner, my fellow citizens, are aspiring despots among yourselves prostituting the name of a Washington to cloak their designs upon your liberties (*The Complete Anti-Federalist,* Storing ed. 2.163).

Some were shocked at the audacity of such attacks on Washington; others found in them further grounds for praise—the man who had risked life and fortune during the war was now risking a possession even more valuable, to himself and to the republic, his "character" and its central importance to a nascent people. That is the realistic light in which Washington viewed his gamble. And he never did worthier service to his country than when he committed himself to the same bark as his fellow delegates, prepared to ride out the storm with them, knowing his presence was crucial to a successful journey, but knowing as well that he would be battered in the process.

This note of sacrifice was necessary to fill out the Enlightenment image of greatness, which called for a surrender to duty, even to death. Washington often risked death during the war, but lived on. It was important, nonetheless, to link him in spirit with those who won the earliest honors of the Revolution, martyrs like Warren and Montgomery, Mercer and Hale, Scammell and Laurens. Even the sea had its oblation—Nicholas Biddle. Some criticized John Trumbull for devoting so many pictures to American deaths and defeat; but his instinct was right, and accorded with popular taste. Since fame was to be won on earth, and the end crowned the work, a noble death was not only a private achievement, but a pledge that the new nation was worth dying for. The best sign that a thing deserved to win was men's willingness to lose for it.

The Revolutionary iconography begins with martyrdom. The moment of sacrifice must be made timeless, kept present to men's minds, so that the republic can live from its own deaths. Samuel Adams created a liturgy around the annual Massacre Day. The first great national monument was ordered from France to commemorate the death of Montgomery at Quebec—Caffiéri designed it, at Franklin's direction, a year after independence was declared. A brave death was the most obvious example of the purchase of honor with praise. Orators sealed the bargain: "Who, that hath worth and merit, would not quit a present uncertain life to live eternally in the memory of present and future ages?" (Royster 32).

Books on the Revolution, down to the time of Irving's *Life of Washington,* saved their finest prose for set pieces on the deaths of heroes. Even John Marshall's sober compilation pauses to say, of John Laurens, that he faced death "with the ardour of a young soldier, whose courage seems to have partaken largely of that romantic spirit which youth and enthusiasm produce in a fearless mind" (4.575). Death was the test and final proof of heroism. As Addison's collaborator, Richard Steele, put it in his 1701 booklet *The Christian Hero:*

Yet, without following them [heroes] through all the handsome incidents and passages of life, we may know them well enough in miniature by beholding them only in their manner of dying. For in those last minutes, the soul and the body both collect all their force either bravely to oppose the enemy or gracefully receive the conqueror death.

The painters of the Enlightenment celebrated a virtuous death as man's greatest triumph. Jacques-Louis David made his Socrates (Figure 20) a human Zeus, judging life and death from his superior vantage point. The timeless moment of death is presented as a frieze spread across the surface of the canvas, while those forced to live on are dwindling down time's tunnel on the left. Plato, sitting at the foot of his master's bed, is at the axis of time and eternity, the one who must carry the message of that death to the ignoble world that caused it. The fact that Plato is shown as the *aged* teacher, not the young disciple, shows that the moment of death lives in his memory (and therefore in ours). The full tragedy of the picture is expressed in Plato's fallen head and weary pose, its contrast with the lifted head and hand of Socrates. The picture poses the question of Socrates' last words in the *Apology:* "The time has come to part, I to die, and you to live. And which of us goes the happier way? That is unknown but to god."

Richard Steele had tried to refashion Christian heroism in Plutarchan terms: "Why is it that the heathen struts, the Christian sneaks, in our imagination?" David reverses the process, incorpo-

Du 13. juillet 1793
Marie anne Charlotte
Corday au citoyen
Marat.
il suffit que je sois
bien Malheureuse
pour avoir Droit
a votre bienveillance.

À MARAT,
DAVID.

L'AN — DEUX

rating Christian pathos in scenes of classical sacrifice. Even in the *Death of Socrates,* there is a hint of the Christian Eucharist, as a teacher takes the cup, in the midst of his grieving disciples, while coming to terms with his own death and promising that his words will remain with them.

The Christian reference is more pointed in David's *Death of Marat* (Figure 50). Here the face canted toward us resembles Christ's in the Michelangelo *Pietà.* The fallen right arm resembles that in many deposition pictures, going back at least to Raphael's time (Figure 51), where the pathos is derived from contrast with the wonder-working right arm of Last Judgments and miracle pictures. In Raphael's painting, omnipotence has been drained from the dead man's arm. Yet in the arm's very surrender of power lies a promise of resurrection. That hand will again be raised in judgment. In David's secular pietà, the writing arm that served the revolution has performed a labor that lives. The box that served as Marat's writing desk has become a monument, the humble sign of heroic duties performed to the end. (David also highlighted the hero's arm in his *Death of Lepeletier,* where the wound in the dead man's side is even more evocative of deposition pictures—Figure 52.)

Thomas Jefferson was intrigued by deposition-pietà scenes as a type (he called it the "descent"). He hung two examples side by side in his parlor, and referred to a third example of the genre in his catalogue of paintings. One of his paintings, properly a pietà, was painted on wood by Francis Floris: "the body of Jesus is reclined on the ground, the head & shoulders supported in the lap of his mother, who with four other women from Galilee are [sic] weeping over him." The other is a copy of Van Dyck's deposition. After describing it, Jefferson adds: "see Rubens' management of the same subject 3. Manuel du Museum. 483" (1809 Catalogue, numbers 51 and 52).

It is appropriate that Jefferson should be interested in the iconographic treatment of Jesus' death, since the application of

50　Jacques-Louis David, *Assassination of Marat* (1793)
. . . the writer's right arm stilled

51   Raphael, the Baglioni *Deposition* (1507)
. . . right arm to be raised in judgment

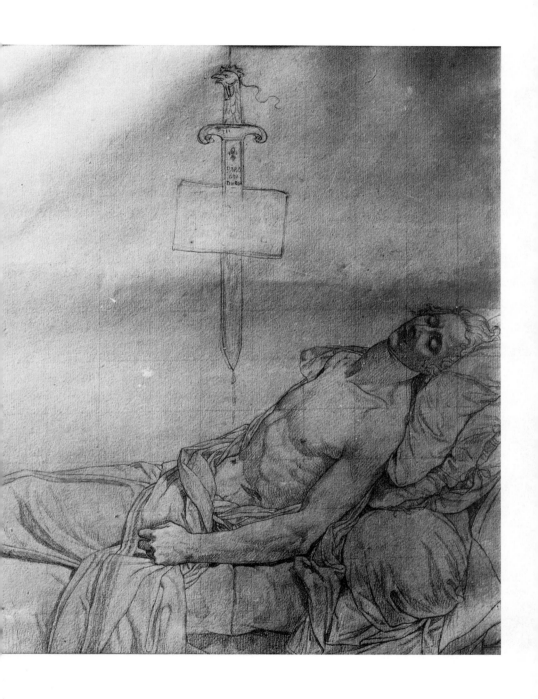

52 Engraving from Jacques-Louis David, *Death of Lepeletier* (1793)
. . . the pietà wound

53 Benjamin West, *Death of General Wolfe* (1770)
. . . an Indian as Virgin at the Cross

54 John Trumbull, *Death of General Warren at Bunker's Hill* (1786)
. . . cheating death of victory

that type to modern historical subjects was an American invention,
as Charles Mitchell demonstrated in 1944. Benjamin West first em-
ployed the schema in his 1770 *Death of General Wolfe* (Figure 53),
where the flag arbitrarily raised behind the hero serves as a cross,
and the ministering figures are in the position of mourners who
have lowered Jesus from it. David was impressed by this, as by
other innovations of West; but Americans were especially known
for glorifying political martyrs in this mode. John Trumbull based
all his death scenes on it. The Raphael pose is repeated in his
Death of General Warren at the Battle of Bunker's Hill (Figure 54).
Sometimes, for variety, Trumbull reverses the direction of the
body—in his classical *Priam Returning with the Body of Hector,* as
in his *Death of General Montgomery in the Attack on Quebec* (Figure
55).

55 John Trumbull, *Death of General Montgomery in the
Attack on Quebec* (1786)
. . . apocalyptic descent

The duty that led men to their own death was often seen as less wrenching than a harsher duty that made them send others to death. The great exemplar of this duty was Brutus, who condemned his own sons as traitors. Machiavelli wrote:

Not less necessary than useful was Brutus' severity in maintaining in Rome the liberty he had gained there. It is an instance striking among recorded events that the father should sit on the judgment seat and not merely condemn his sons to death but be present at their deaths (*Discourses*, Gilbert ed. 424).

David did not paint the moment of judgment or of execution, but that when his sons were carried into his own grieving household (Figure 41). Like Plato, Brutus must live on after the shattering death. On the left (male) side of the picture, Brutus has been contemplating his tragic decision, seated in shadow under the demanding goddess of Rome. A moment earlier, his head was on his hand, his body tied in a knot of concentration, even his feet twisted together—the pose from Michelangelo's Sistine Isaiah. But the head of Michelangelo's prophet is lifted and turned to his right by a whisper of inspiration drawing him out of himself. Brutus' head is jerked to the left (our right) by the keening of the women, who can see the bodies from which he is shut off by the shrine of the goddess. He sits, like the statue above him, displaced from the flow of emotion and life around the dead men's return.

This work was exhibited in the first year of the French Revolution; and it has an accidental tie with the American Revolution. One of David's sources was the 1788 play by Vittorio Alfieri, *Bruto Primo,* which ends with the people crying that Brutus is the god of Rome, to which Brutus replies, "And the unhappiest man ever born" (Starobinski 111). Alfieri dedicated his play to George Washington, the modern Brutus (*"Al chiarissimo e libero Uomo il Generale Washington"*). For us, I suppose, there is something unsettling in these works. Enlightenment authors and artists showed an al-

most fierce glee in the sacrifice of one's children to the state—
which suggests the language of modern statism, of totalitarianism.
It is enough to give a sinister, if anachronistic, meaning to all the
fasces in eighteenth-century art. The Terror shows that such fears
are, at least partly, merited.

Yet David has just put on canvas the conflicts of neoclassical
theater; like Addison and Voltaire, he "bourgeoisifies" the conflict
between a code of honor and family affection in the aristocratic
worlds of Corneille and Racine. If revolutionaries wanted to replace the aristocrats, they had to outsuffer them, make Everyman
a Polyeucte:

J'ai de l'ambition, mais plus noble et plus belle (Polyeucte 4.3).

Now the *citizen* can have honor, if he or she is willing to accept a
code of sacrifice. A leveling duty invades the home, where affection had differentiated roles. In David's painting, the other members of Brutus' family—wife, daughters, dead sons—are all equal
in the eyes of the state, all citizens, all accountable to Rome. David
added daughters to the Brutus story to increase the quantity of
familial grief. In *Mort de César,* Voltaire even made Brutus Caesar's
natural son, so that the clash of private and public duties would
be starker.

This raw assertion of the state must be seen in context, not
only as spreading to others the monopoly on honor held by nobles
and aristocrats, but as breaking the hold of court and church on
affections that must be transferred to the polity's new machinery.
A wrenching of emotional ties was involved, even before the melo-
dramatic family scenes of Addison and David were invented—
they are, in fact, individual concentrations of the conflict's larger
social shape. The displacing of the Virgin's statue with an image
of the martyred Marat is a little parable of the war going on in
men's hearts; and the revolution that struggled hardest to clear

away the past with its Terror is also the one that lapsed back toward established religion. Washington seems, perhaps, too stern to us, inflexible in his sense of duty. But there was no ferocity in that devotion, no touch of the hysterical, as in Robespierre; partly because his classical ideals were adopted for their own sake, not out of a suspicion that religion's hold was unshakable. Virginians could afford to be more tolerant than Parisians.

For Europeans, Washington was Cincinnatus from the moment he resigned his war commission in 1783. When David supervised the painting of a copy from his famous *Oath of the Horatii*, he softened the fierce call to duty that painting had first expressed in 1785. He put, under the swords, a plow that had not appeared in the original (Figure 12). The sons are called from the plow, and must return to it, like modern Cincinnati. The painting, despite this alteration (and the addition of a spindle on the female side of the picture) is still fierce in its definition of duty to the state. David had earlier planned an even harsher moment of the story for illustration. After the three Horatii have vowed to defend their country against the three Curiatii, two of the Roman sons fall in battle; the third returns to find one sister weeping for the Curiatius she loved—and he kills her. The father then defends him against the charge of murder; she should not have put her love above the state's interests. Though David abandoned an earlier sketch of the father defending his son, the outcome of the story is adumbrated in his painting of the oath. The arrangement of shadow had been clotted in *Brutus*—the father and his goddess seated in the dark, buried in awful duty, while the light is mockingly clear over the women's protest at death. On the Horatii, light is shed more evenly; but one son is boldly lit, the other two more dimly, a literal "foreshadowing." On the weeping-female side of the picture, the sister who must die is, like the brother who will kill her, nearest to us. Within their own home and family, the two are paired as foes; his raised hand proleptically fells her. One sword, from that fasces of them held by the father, will kill a Roman as well as the Alban challengers.

Starobinski, discussing this painting, finds it the emblem of a spiritual movement:

The year 1789 saw the taking of many oaths. These included George Washington's oath of allegiance to the American Constitution on April 30; the Tennis Court Oath on June 20, when the deputies of the Third Estate declared themselves a National Assembly and swore not to separate until they had given France a constitution; and the oaths of the National Guards . . . Marriages were often celebrated before the altar to the *Patrie,* thus combining the loyalties of the spouse and of the citizen. And every flag, with its legend, "Liberty or Death," was a reminder of an oath (Starobinski 102).

It may seem odd to us that Alfieri associates Washington with Brutus, that Starobinski places him in spirit with the Horatii; but there was a severity in Washington, admired by the Enlightenment, that helps explain the lack of an easy affection for him in our day. Without knowing much about the harsh classical heroes, he could by instinct capture the spirit of their acts. Cato not only refused to profit from his wars, but used the office of quaestor to restore financial discipline and credit to Rome (Plutarch 16–18). Pericles sacrificed his own house when calling citizens from the countryside to abandon their homes and take shelter in Athens (Thucydides 2.13), as Publicola destroyed his own house when citizens called it too imposing (Plutarch 10). Augustus sent his only child, a beloved daughter, into exile when her conduct threatened the state (Tacitus *Annals* 3.24).

Washington reproduced the spirit of these men in his life. Like Cato, he insisted on national credit, from the days of his "legacy" through all the assaults on Hamilton's financial plan. Like Pericles and Publicola, he was ready to sacrifice his estate when the British threatened it with their ships' guns on the Potomac. The first time this happened, the overseer at Mount Vernon sent out grain and supplies to placate the enemy. When Washington heard of this, he wrote instructions to let the house be leveled to the ground rather than repeat such an offering (GW 22.14–15).

Like Augustus, Washington banished from his presence, for a time (he knew not how long), one to whom he felt bound by deep ties of affection. To maintain his neutrality policy, Washington refused any interview with French visitors that could be construed as taking sides in their revolutionary struggle. This meant that he had to turn away the Viscount of Noailles, Lafayette's brother-in-law and a veteran of Yorktown (Freeman 7.63). He followed the same course with Talleyrand (ibid. 227). He even forced himself to the same conduct with regard to Lafayette himself. After Lafayette was imprisoned, his wife begged Washington to intervene with pleas for his release. As a private citizen he helped her financially; but he left it to Jefferson, as Secretary of State, to express American regard for Lafayette in a way that would not insult the French Government. Then, when George Washington Lafayette, one hero's son named for another, arrived in Boston with his tutor, Washington wrote that he could not see him, that the boy should stay in the North and attend Harvard. Only after an eight-month delay, when Congress had invited the young Lafayette to the federal city, did Washington receive him into his home (ibid. 304, 323, 395; Flexner 4.261–64). Private emotion had always to wait on public duty while Washington was in office.

He showed a similar rigor when he refused to tell Edmund Randolph, his Secretary of State, about the charges against him— since telling him could have endangered the Jay Treaty (Freeman 7.287–98).

The inflexible demands Washington made on himself and others have intimidated or chilled later generations; but in a perilous time they were the steadying force for an entire national experiment. His singleness of purpose sustained his Army in a war of tactical losses; there was never any doubt, that, in the midst of

56   Edward Savage, *Washington's Family* (1796)
. . . sunrise over the republic

defeat, he meant to prevail. If the British should win, Washington
would hide in the West (GW 4.359), not return to Mount Vernon
(ibid. 14.147), since "I shall neither ask for, nor expect any favor
from his most gracious Majesty." Others doubted, hoped, changed
course, or hesitated. Once Washington set his purpose, he left his
home for good and lived only for his Army. "My life is grafted on
the fate of Rome."

It is hard to fix the exact place on the scale of republican
severity that Washington was able to make his own. Far short of
the brutal ideal presented in some of David's paintings, Washington's code is still so *entirely* public as to seem uncongenial now.
Even when Washington is presented in domestic surroundings,
the note of duty is sounded—as in Edward Savage's painting of
the Washingtons at home (Figure 56), a picture that became very
popular in its engraved form. Finished in the year of the Farewell

Address, the work accomplishes what Mario Praz thought impossible, the *political* use of a "conversation piece." Washington has given up public life, taken off his sword, and begun to read. Like Canova, Savage conflates the two retirements—from the Army and from the presidency. Washington still wears his uniform, but he has retired at a time when the federal city is being raised, just up the Potomac from Mount Vernon. We see the river in the background, and trace its course with Martha on the map she has spread across her husband's interrupted reading. She points to the Capitol site. But Washington, who never lived in the city named for him, is a spectator now. The future belongs to the young Americans who will follow him, typified in the couple's grandson, who stands by the pillar of state and has been studying the globe. The sun is rising over the Potomac, as the republic takes life from the Founder's surrender of power.

This public code even in domestic matters was expressed by the original republicans of our Revolution. In his 1786 essay, "Of the Mode of Education Proper in a Republic," Benjamin Rush wrote:

Our country includes family, friends, and property, and should be preferred to them all. Let our pupil be taught that he does not belong to himself, but that he is public property. Let him be taught to love his family, but let him be taught, at the same time, that he must forsake and even forget them when the welfare of his country requires it. He must watch for the state as if its liberties depended upon his vigilance alone.

In 1776, John Adams used similar language, writing to Joseph Warren:

Public virtue is the only foundation of Republics. There must be a positive passion for the public good, the public interest.

Ironically, Adams remains lovable to us for his private side, his prickly spontaneity and humor. Jefferson said of him, "He never acted on any system, but was always governed by the feeling of the moment." Washington, by contrast, *always* acted on a system, which makes him less winningly vulnerable than other great men of the founding time. Jefferson himself, filling pages with bitter accusations against his enemies, reminds me of John Henry Newman in Chesterton's description: "a naked man bearing a naked sword." Madison, so nervous that he thought himself an epileptic, needed his Dolley's nursing. Hamilton, touchy about his private honor, was publicly too voluble. But Washington, not leaning on others, kept his own counsel, at a cool remove. Color seems to drain from him into his contemporaries, leaving him white as marble. Yet what shines like marble over the years, looked, close up, like a granite whose toughness was the one thing requisite—as at the Battle of Princeton. William Rush said that the sheer force of Washington's presence turned the tide of that encounter, as the fleeing Pennsylvanians formed ranks around him. The shared risk, the participation in joint sacrifice, left no doubt in the minds of those present that Washington's resolve was joined to humane concerns.

One of those present at the battle was Charles Willson Peale. He took sketches of the actual scene, and might have been expected to render the battle accurately. Instead, he painted it in allegorical form, making it almost domestic in its tenderness, emphasizing the sacrifice needed to prevail in war. Compared with Peale's large painting (which now hangs in Nassau Hall, at Princeton), even John Trumbull's smaller depiction of the event looks repertorial (Figure 29). Yet Trumbull took many liberties with the accounts he received. Washington never saw General Mercer, to the rescue of whose men he rode. Mercer was bayonetted five times, then carried from the field. Trumbull brings Washington up behind the dying Mercer at the very moment when the latter's guns are being taken and his forces scattered. The aim is to *connect* the sacrifice of Mercer with the achievement of the victory. In this

57   Antoine-Jean Gros, *Napoleon at Jaffa* (1804)
. . . reanimating the dead

"pietà," a resurrection, a rescue takes place between the recumbent figure and the "cross" of smoke-wreathed tree. If martyrs give life to the republic, they do it through the actions of Washington, who comes to vindicate their sacrifice.

Antoine-Jean Gros painted Napoleon bringing rescue out of crisis, life out of death, in battlefield scenes. His most striking treatment of this death-and-resurrection theme is Bonaparte visting the plague-ridden at Jaffa (Figure 57), which deals with the end of the Egyptian campaign, Napoleon's first major defeat. The plague-stricken French soldiers are dying without the comfort, even, of a tangible foe to grapple with. In the right foreground a doctor slumps, defeated. Those on the left of the picture are suffering the agonies of the damned (the staring figure with his head on his hands is taken from Michelangelo's *Last Judgment*). But, in the light, where Napoleon moves fearlessly among the sick (in contrast to his gagging and reluctant officers), people struggle back to their feet, revivified by his animating presence. This is a secular miracle scene, which demonstrates Napoleon's effect on his followers even at their darkest hour.

For Napoleon to be turned into a Christlike miracle worker shows the ambivalence of the French Revolution toward religious symbols. By contrast, the pietàs of the American artists are secularizations with an entirely immanent logic; the resurrection is to fame for the martyr and victory for the republic. So Peale, in his work for Nassau Hall (Plate 1), makes Washington tower out of the subsiding Mercer's death. Trumbull had used the features of Mercer's son as his model for the dead general's features; but he aged them appropriately to achieve verisimilitude. Peale, who had adopted Mercer's deaf-mute son and taught him to paint, retained the youth of his model. Like David painting Joseph Barra, Peale meant to summarize the sacrifice of all the Revolution's young martyrs. He captures in a single image the repeated lyrics over fallen warriors in Timothy Dwight's *Conquest of Canaan:*

> Far from the fight, despoiled of helm and shield,
> Slept beauteous Irad on the mournful field.
> Deaf to the groans and careless of the cries,
> His hair soft-whistling o'er his half-shut eyes.
> On either side his lifeless arms were spread
> And blood ran round him from the countless dead.
> Even there, two warriors rushing o'er the plain,
> O'er crimson torrents and o'er piles of slain,
> Stopped when the lovely form arose to sight,
> Surveyed his charms and wished no more the fight (8.499–508).

But where, in the poem, soldiers are softened from their fighting mood, Washington rises in Peale's painting like a phoenix from the fire of Mercer's death—or like the eagle of the republic

58 William Rush, *The Schuylkill Chained* (1825)
. . . tamed nature frees the eagle

from the agony of tamed nature in William Rush's *The Schuylkill Chained* (Figure 58). Here death and resurrection are linked as a single act. Peale uses the pietà formula for the first and last time, with the flag again doing service as a cross. The attendants on Mercer—lowering him, as it were, from the cross—have a reverence and awareness of mystery far more intimate, less theatrical, than the mourners in West's work or Trumbull's. Washington turns toward Nassau Hall and the victory, transmuting loss to gain, death to life. He guarantees the dead their glory. As Dwight put it:

> Thus hung with wounds, a prey to savage steel
> In Princeton's fields the gallant Mercer fell.
> When first his native realm her sons decreed
> In slavery's chains with want and woe to bleed,
> Check'd, through his bosom fond remembrance ran
> The cause of freedom was the cause of man.
> In that fair cause he bared his manly breast,
> The friend, the hope, the champion, of the oppressed.
> From height to height on glory's pinion rose,
> Bless'd by his friends and praised by generous foes.
> Swift flew the shaft; the eagle ceased to rise,
> And mourning millions traced him down the skies (8.543–54).

59   Jacques-Louis David, *Lavoisier and His Wife* (1788)
. . . light on the sacred progeny

The task of the republic was to be worthy of its martyrs; and Washington's claim on his fellows came from the fact that he so clearly had the disinterested virtue they died for. He served for no pay, no power; only for praise. Benjamin Rush was right to contrast him with Napoleon in this respect. The Napoleon of the Gros painting *gives* life, saves men, bestows meaning on their death. But Peale is telling us that Washington *receives* life from the martyrs, more animated by their virtues than animating others.

David has shown, in the *Horatii,* how the duty of the citizen can rend the family, can kill loved ones so the Public Thing will prevail. Peale's surprisingly intimate military painting, with its touches of family piety, makes Washington a father who does not exact death from his sons but avenges a death freely given. David could depict republican virtues as a binding force in the family (Figure 59), as well as a disruptive one. But he never joined the two concepts as persuasively as that is accomplished in Peale's neglected masterpiece. No other political work of the time shows such tenderness at the heart of republican severity.

XII

HEAD AND HEART

> The generous plan of power deliver'd down,
> From age to age, by your renown'd Fore-fathers.
> —Addison, *Cato* 3.5.

IN THE PITTSBURGH *Gazette* for November 10, 1787, Hugh Henry Brackenridge portrayed, with mocking glee, the quandary of those attacking the new Constitution despite the "great names" favoring that draft:

> In this case, 'twill give much ado,
> To overpower the names against us,
> Although we take the greatest pains t' us,
> But let us do what can be done.
> For instance, as to Washington,
> Say his skill lies wholly in arms,
> And care of his Virginia farms;
> But neither knows of state affairs,
> No more than buff'lo does of prayers;
> And as to Franklin say he fails
> In judgment as his age prevails.

It was appropriate that both of America's greatest names should be linked with each other and with the new government. Washington was the Founder *par excellence;* but it is a measure of his greatness, in the eyes of contemporaries, that he (and he alone)

195

could bear comparison with the man whose fame was already secure before the Revolution began. For many, both in America and abroad, Franklin *was* the Enlightenment. His bust was one of the few modern ones considered worthy of inclusion among those of the ancient heroes. In America, he was considered such an awesome phenomenon that Charles Willson Peale hoped, with his taxidermist's skills, to preserve Franklin's body for display in his museum (as the British later preserved Jeremy Bentham).

Washington, too, was a man of the Enlightenment, a promoter of science and education; one of his dearest hopes was for the establishment of a national university. He experimented with a plow of his own design (*Diaries* 1.255–58, 263–65) and with new plows imported from England (GW 29.232). He systematically tested the potential of various native grapes for the making of wine (GW 27.55). He sent rare-bird carcasses to be mounted in Peale's museum (GW 29.139, 163, 178). He manifested the "philosophical" (scientific) curiosity that is the mark of his time: ordering a sleigh to get him through the snows of Newburgh, he asked

upon Philosophical, Mechanical, or practical principles, is it best to have the Sliders (excepting always the curve in front) a little circular, or quite straight? The longer the bearing the greater the friction; the shorter, the weight is confined to a smaller space of the sliders, and consequently the compressure greater; as a part in one case, bears what the whole does in the other (GW 25.439).

Washington's own view of the age he lived in is best expressed in his hopes for America as he said farewell to the states' governors at the end of the war:

The foundation of our Empire was not laid in the gloomy age of Ignorance and Superstition, but at an Epocha when the rights of mankind were better understood and more clearly defined, than at any former period, the researches of the human mind, after social happiness, have been carried to a great extent, the Treasures of knowledge, acquired by the labours of Philosophers, Sages and Legislatures, through a long succession of years, are laid open for our use, and their collected wisdom may be happily applied in the Establishment of our forms of Government (GW 26.485).

But Washington, whatever his friendly feelings for science, was not a scientist himself; and the sense that Washington and Franklin expressed the *entire* character of American achievement led to a rough "division of labor" in expressing the nation's gratitude to its greatest men. Washington was the man of virtue, of public spirit and personal dedication. Franklin was the man of wisdom, of a vivid curiosity made stable with good sense. Together, they gave the Revolution its heart and its head. As Pennsylvanians were singing in 1788 (Freeman 6.147):

> Great Washington shall rule the land,
> While Franklin's counsel guides his hand.

Poor John Adams grumbled at the monopoly the two men seemed to be establishing over all the heroism of their time. He wrote to Benjamin Rush in 1790:

The history of our Revolution will be . . . that Dr. Franklin's electric rod smote the earth and out sprung General Washington. That Franklin electrised him with his rod, and thence-forward these two conducted all the policy, negotiations, legislatures, and war.

A sense of the complementarity of the heroes' labors had reached England as early as 1783, when the Revolution was just completed. Joseph Banks, president of the Royal Society, wrote Franklin from London:

General Washington has we are told Cincinnatus like return'd to cultivate his garden now the emancipated States have no farther occasion for his sword. How much more pleasure would it be for you to return to your more entertaining more elevated and I will say more useful pursuit of Philosophy. The head of the Philosopher guides the hand of the farmer to more abundant crops than nature or instinct or unguided reason could have produced.

Though Banks seems to give preeminence to the head, it was more common in the 1780s to honor the heart. The moral sense revealed the goals of morality to men, through his sentiments and affections. Reason merely chose means to the ends the heart established. As Hume wrote in his *Inquiry Concerning the Principles of Morals:*

It appears evident that the ultimate ends of human actions can never, in any case, be accounted for by *reason,* but recommend themselves entirely to the sentiments and affections of mankind, without any dependance on the intellectual faculties (Nidditch ed. 293).

As students of Voltaire, Diderot, and Rousseau are always reminding us, the "age of reason" was really an age of sentiment. In this, too, Washington was a man of his age. When he established the first general decoration in the American Army, the Purple Heart, it was not (as it became in the twentieth century) an award available to all soldiers wounded in the line of duty. Only privates and noncommissioned officers could win the original "Badge of Military Merit," a cloth-shaped heart sewn over the man's actual heart, which allowed him to "pass all guards and sentinels which officers are permitted to do." The symbol was not of heart's blood shed, but of virtue proceeding from the heart. Limiting the award to nonofficers was meant to indicate that great virtue can be shown regardless of rank—that, in Washington's words, "the road to glory in a patriot army and a free country is thus open to all" (GW 24.488). Washington himself cannot, therefore, be "demoted" by considering him the heart of the Revolution, as Franklin was the head.

Even during the Revolutionary War, before Washington's greatest achievements—his resignation, "legacy," reform of the Cincinnati, service to the Constitution, presidency, and Farewell Address—Jefferson put Washington's name first when maintaining, to a French audience, that America could produce greatness:

In war we have produced a Washington, whose memory will be adored while liberty shall have votaries, whose name shall triumph over time, and will in future ages assume its just station among the most celebrated worthies of the world (*Notes on the State of Virginia,* Query VI).

The second name Jefferson offered was, inevitably, Franklin's:

In physics we have produced a Franklin, than whom no one of the present age has made more important discoveries, nor has enriched philosophy with more, or more ingenious solutions of the phenomena of nature (ibid.).

Not surprisingly, Jefferson paired Houdon's busts of Washington and Franklin in his "most honorable suite" (Figure 32), as Houdon had paired them in his own studio (Figure 33), or Morse had in his painting of Lafayette (Figure 40). When William Rush was commissioned to do a life-size statue of Washington (Figure 45), he made it a companion in pose to the marble Franklin that Lazzarini had sculpted for the Library Company (Figure 46). The heroes expressed something in conjunction that neither could embody on his own. And the link between their destinies and their country's fate seems to have been felt by Washington. At the time when he was debating whether to risk his "character" on the struggle for a new Constitution, he expressed the same concern for Franklin (GW 28.308–9, 338–39). He described Franklin's effort in the same terms used for the contemplation of his own: "He has again embarked on a troubled ocean" (ibid. 308).

The joint stature of the two men, and the complementarity of their deeds, is aptly symbolized by the fact that they (and only they) achieved a consistent iconography as classical heroes—Cincinnatus in Washington's case, Prometheus in Franklin's. Other images were considered for both men. In some ways, it was (for a time) argued, Washington resembled Moses, or Joshua, or Fabius. But only one "forebear" expressed the totality of his virtue: Cincinnatus. In the same way, Franklin was called, at various times, Nestor or Mentor. But only Prometheus presented him as both the tamer of nature and the political liberator, the two aspects joined in Turgot's famous line about Franklin:

Eripuit coelo fulmen, sceptrumque tyrannis.

He tore from heaven lightning, scepters from kings.

In early portraits, from the 1760s, only the first of these achievements could be shown, before Franklin's participation in the Revolution. Two paintings especially, through copies and engravings, associated Franklin indelibly with his electrical apparatus. Benjamin Wilson showed many people, through James McArdell's mezzotint, how Franklin tamed the lightning with his book *Electrical Experiments* (Figure 60). And Mason Chamberlain's painting, seen here in Edward Fisher's engraving (Figure 61), showed how Franklin rigged up bells that would ring according to the intensity with which his own home's lightning rod had been struck. This controlled use of nature's energy is contrasted with the untamed power of the lightning bolt in the background, which rends the pediment from a classical building. The association of Franklin with his scientific apparatus was the strongest visual image some Americans had of "the thinker." When Jefferson was elected President in 1800, before citizens at large had a clear visual image of him, an engraver thought the easiest way to suggest his intellectual stature was simply to put him in Dr. Franklin's laboratory (Figure 62).

During the Revolution, the *political* aspect of Franklin's Promethean gifts completed the image of him. Fragonard, for instance, illustrated Turgot's line by showing, on the left (male) side of his drawing, Mars defeating the tyrants; and, on the (female) right side, Minerva deflecting the lightning (Figure 24). Martial heart and scientific head were celebrated in this propaganda for the Franco-American alliance. A chaster depiction of Franklin's

60   McArdell mezzotint of Benjamin Wilson painting *Benjamin Franklin* (1761)

      . . . light on apparatus defeats the lightning

61   Fisher mezzotint of Mason Chamberlain painting *Benjamin Franklin* (1763)
. . . the laboratory uses what ravages the countryside

62   Cornelius Tiebout, *Thomas Jefferson* (1801)
. . . if a philosopher, then a Franklin

spirit, seen as an antique nude, appears on Augustin Dupré's medal struck in honor of the new Prometheus (Figure 25). A temple is preserved, on the left, by Franklin's lightning rod; and tyrannical baubles are cast down on the right. Jefferson had one of these medals hanging in Monticello's little shrine of American heroes (1809 Catalogue, p. 10).

Late in his life, Benjamin West designed a Promethean picture of Franklin for the two men's shared city of Philadelphia, though he never went beyond the painted study for it (Figure 26). Here the angels of the spheres, who attend on God in medieval cosmogonies—the same genii who are swept along in the robes of Michelangelo's creating deity on the Sistine ceiling—are domesticated. One even wears the Indian feathers of the genius of America. Rather than sing in the motion of the spheres, these "angels" are intimately involved in the experiments of Franklin's "heavenly" laboratory. Here we see for the first time a depiction of Franklin's kite experiment, which was *not* part of his earliest iconography. The learned audience Franklin addressed in his works knew that he was more a theoretician than a tinkerer, though a later audience, fond of the "Poor Richard" image, would associate him more readily with *Popular Mechanics* than with Newton's *Principia*. Having suggested the kite experiment, Franklin did not get around to performing it until European readers of his works had done so—and even then the experiment was done so casually that we cannot tell exactly where or when it took place.

Not the least resemblance between Washington and Franklin is the way later legends trivialized the men by simultaneous processes of inflation and deflation. Franklin's kite has become a cartoon emblem of the man, as has Washington's hatchet for the cherry tree. And Fragonard's apotheosis chills or amuses a modern audience, much as Greenough's Washington does. We have lost

63   Sandro Botticelli, *Saint Augustine* (c. 1485)
     . . . light streams through the universe

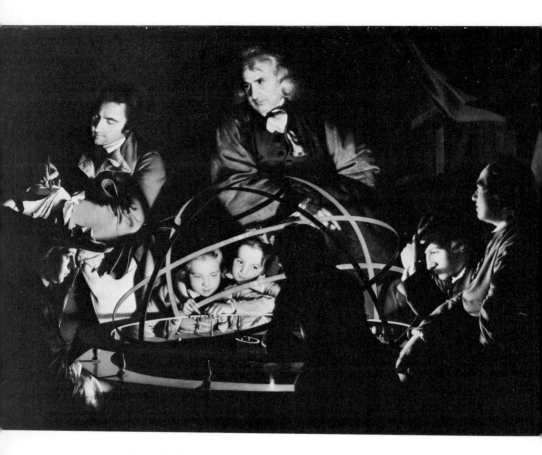

64   Joseph Wright of Derby, *Philosopher and Orrery* (c. 1764–66)
. . . light immanent, haloing humans

the historical framework for work like West's, in which an "apotheosis" of Barralet's sort (Figure 6) was meant as an *inverted* apotheosis, the lifting up of the deliberately lowly virtues of the citizen. In the same way, the cosmic effects around West's Franklin are meant as anti-cosmogonies, a secularization of creation myths and heavenly inspiration. These pictures are telling us that Franklin did something more than tame the atmosphere; he brought light into the center of human life. Just as Cato's virtue was an earned trait, not a divine gift, so Franklin's wisdom was won by observation, not shed on him from above.

A secularization of Washington's Moses image was necessary in the republic. So was a secularization of the wisdom imagery around Franklin. In Botticelli's *Saint Augustine,* divine light streams on and through the universe to reach man's mind (Figure 63). Jean Starobinski says it was part of the Enlightenment's program to make light immanent, not invasive, at the popular level (43–45, 242–43). All "Sun Kings" and solar deities had to be replaced by luminous laws at work in man's daily life. The great secularizer of light was Joseph Wright of Derby, whose orrery takes the Augustinian model of the Universe and puts it at the center of popular and learned study (Figure 64). The machinery of the universe is no longer permeated by an outside light. A candle at the center replaces the sun, for the purpose of man's study—just as Franklin's "genii" descend from their spheres, in the West painting, and participate in his experiments. The orrery was a kind of holy object in the Enlightenment: Jefferson made a cult of Rittenhouse's, and Washington was taken on pilgrimage to see Joseph Pope's at Harvard (*Diaries* 5.481–83).

Ronald Poulson noticed how Wright took the conventional nativity scene, where light emanates from the divine baby, and turned it into a blacksmith's forge, where human labor fans a light for shaping new things. In the same way, David makes of Lavoisier and his wife a new "holy family," where the play of light on and in the chemical apparatus gives off a glow of the new science (Figure 59). The offspring of such a family is the shining knowledge husband and wife provide to a revolutionary era. This is the significance of the optical effects of light playing on Franklin's apparatus in the Wilson and Chamberlin paintings (Figures 61, 62). The Promethean image of Franklin is more grandiose than Norman Rockwell's *Saturday Evening Post* one, which has replaced it for our time. But the point of the early paintings was that Prometheus brought fire *down;* not only used it, but demystified it. If we no longer feel the need to bring the light from an empty heaven, that is because the Enlightenment won its battle. Franklin so *thoroughly* brought the fire to earth that we forget it ever had so far to travel.

Fragonard's image of Prometheus has receded from our view, leaving us a trivialized "Ben" of the kite story. The very name is a symptom. Franklin was more often referred to by contemporaries as "Dr. Franklin" than was Samuel Johnson as "Dr. Johnson"—with good cause: he had more honorary doctorates, as well as more honors in every sense. In an age that joined simplicity and dignity, the founders addressed each other as "Sir." It was against his undeniable international stature that Franklin asserted a deliberate plainness, in his prose as well as his dress, without losing republican gravity. It took him some time to shed his wig, but he finally arrived at the plain "Quaker" dress that resembles Washington's "second mourning" attire as President. Benjamin West, of Quaker descent himself and the celebrator of William Penn, put a plainly dressed Franklin in the center of his picture of the American peace commissioners presenting the treaty that ended the Revolutionary War (Figure 65). Franklin, most assured of posterity's attention, looks out at the audience as if presenting the meaning of the action directly to us, across time. The man of peace is at the center of this scene, as Washington was at the center of the war.

Though Franklin was not literally a Quaker, he saw that the values perceived in Quaker plainness, by *philosophes* like Voltaire, resembled the virtues needed by citizens of the republic. West praised such virtue in his painting of *Penn's Treaty,* another of those secularizing pictures that gave the Enlightenment its revised iconography (Figure 66). One source of the painting is Masaccio's *Tribute Money,* in which Christ works a miracle to prevent conflict with the civil authorities (Figure 67). The mural has a triptych's arrangement, though it is painted on a single surface—the two side episodes are separated from the central group in time as well as space, that on the left happening after the central command, and that on the right happening still later. The miraculous outcome, made certain by Christ's central gesture, is worked out around him.

By contrast, Penn "works peace" through an entirely natural process of fair dealing with his fellows. Human brotherhood, not divine authority, makes the wilderness blossom with good works. The triptych arrangement breaks down, along with other social divisions. Penn is modestly off-center, sharing space with the Indians. Homely genre details, such as the nursing Indian woman, reduce the awesomeness of the scene, making it a large outdoor conversation piece. The Quakers do not command with

65　Benjamin West, *American Peace Commissioners* (1783)
. . . Franklin the "Quaker" of a new order

66 Benjamin West, *Penn's Treaty with the Indians* (c. 1771)
. . . peace through yielding

67 Masaccio, *St. Peter and the Tribute Money* (1428)
. . . peace through miracle

supernatural authority. They win by deferring. Parson Weems drew the scene in his *Life of Penn:*

"Now, brothers, lift up your eyes and see, here, the good things which the Great Spirit has given us to bring to you." Here the English sailors, with their usual alacrity, opened out their ready bales of clothes, their true blues and fiery crimsons and flaming reds, stretching them along in all their dazzling colors on the grass. And then, as by magic, they unpacked their boxes of finely painted guns, with shining tomahawks and axes and hoes and knives and other articles of choice British goods, which they also spread out to the best advantage—William Penn, in the meantime, explaining their uses to the Indians, who now, no longer able to keep their seats on the ground, were risen up, crowded around him with uncontrolled curiosity to look and wonder (ch. 18).

West clearly tried to give the American treaty commissioners (Figure 65) the human qualities praised in his *Penn's Treaty;* but he never completed the painting, very likely because his royal patron would not be pleased with a celebration of England's defeat. Nonetheless, the unfinished work had great (if indirect) influence. While West did life studies for it, John Trumbull was staying with him and planning his own series of modern history paintings. The arrangement of the seven main figures in his *Declaration of Independence* (Figure 68) was clearly affected by the composition of West's group of the same number. In both cases, five men face a seated and a standing figure in profile. Where West's unpainted British emissaries would have been stationed, congressional president John Hancock sits in the Trumbull work, and congressional secretary Charles Thomson stands to his right. The men are addressing a text—the draft treaty in West, the committee's draft for a Declaration in Trumbull—that spills over the side of the table. In each work a spokesman stands ready to explain the draft—John Jay in West, Jefferson in Trumbull—while the others strain to listen.

Only two persons—Franklin and Adams—appear in both pictures, and Trumbull's treatment of the two is clearly influenced

68   John Trumbull, *Declaration of Independence* (1787–1820)
. . . rights of man under trophies of war

by West's. Franklin wears his black clothes, white linen, no wig;
and in both cases he is the only figure who looks out at the viewers. John Adams is shown in three-quarters profile, his face, his
clothes, his body treated in the same way by both artists. John
Quincy Adams remembered how, as a boy, he watched West measure his father's calves while doing this painting—was Trumbull
in the atelier that day? If not, he saw the results soon after, and
they left their mark. The principal difference in the treatment of
Adams (besides the standing and seated postures) is the lack of a
wig in the *Declaration*. But a close inspection of the canvas shows

69   Edward Savage, after Robert Edge Pine, *Congress Voting Independence* (c. 1796–1801)
. . . the committee with wigs

the outline of just such a wig as Adams wears in the West painting—it has been painted out. The wigs on the figures behind
Trumbull's group show that he originally painted his drafting
committee as Edward Savage had (Figure 69), with Adams, Jefferson, and Livingston wearing wigs; only the puritan Roger Sher-
man and the "quakerized" Franklin are wigless. As Washington's
and Franklin's simplicity grew more popular, Trumbull effaced the
wigs on three of his main characters. (Hancock and Thomson, like
most of the delegates already painted in the background, had to
retain theirs.)

West placed Franklin in the center of the American group,
which itself takes up the greater part of his painting's space. Trumbull put Franklin in the center of the looser seven-man composi-

70 Jacques-Louis David, Study for *The Oath of the Tennis Court* (1791)
. . . secular Pentecost

tion, where he shares the glow of light around Jefferson's head. Which raises the question of this light's source. There is light, presumably from a window, entering from the left of the scene, striking the heads of the seated and standing figures there and throwing shadows on the floor. This cannot account for the stronger light that glows behind the committee, under the hanging trophies of battle won from the British. This light comes from the upper right of the picture, where no natural source can be imagined.

A "holy light" in this period usually means an *anti*-light of natural splendor, a counterstatement to the heavenly explanations in traditional art. We have seen how the light of wisdom in Botticelli is secularized in, for instance, David's *Lavoisier and His Wife* (Figure 59). The same can be said of Joseph Wright's "nativity" for an industrial age. Another secularization of light was clearly intended in David's drawing for *The Oath of the Tennis Court* (Figure 70). All critics have noticed how the delegates' raised right arms repeat the gesture of David's *Horatii* (Figure 12) on a larger scale. But there is another, subtler reference to be traced in the whipping of the curtains by a strong wind. That wind's activity makes light shine into the chamber; it is clearly the *spiritus* of the Revolution, its afflatus sweeping through old institutions. David has painted a secular Pentecost.

Giotto's and El Greco's paintings of Pentecost show the light of faith shed on each disciple, so that even those who do not share their language must understand these bearers of fire. David celebrates a new unity of humankind, bound together by belief in all men's rights. The unanimity of spirit is reflected in the articulated "mystical body" fashioned from the ingredients of a mob. The mood spreads outside the tennis court, to the crowds at the window, as the enthusiasm of the disciples made them go from the upper room to the people. All men will speak a common language in the dawn of the Revolution's new day.

There is much more technical virtuosity, more bravura of inspiration, in David's drawing than in Trumbull's laboriously completed *Declaration*. But the two share iconographic concerns. Trumbull aptly sheds a secular light around those declaring that all men are equal. Theirs is a work of fraternity that will bind men together, as the fifty-four figures are woven into an orderly pattern to consider Jefferson's fateful words. The note of military peril, struck by the trophies of war, shows that the entire body is ready to pledge its lives, its fortunes, its sacred honor, to the creed of the new age. It is appropriate that the only man looking out at us is the plainclothes Prometheus who domesticated heaven's light by his force of mind.

XIII

THE ROUNDED IMAGE

> Let me advise thee to retreat betimes
> To thy paternal seat, the Sabine field
> Where the great Censor toiled with his own hands,
> And all our frugal ancestors were blest
> In humble virtues and a rural life.
> There live retired, pray for the peace of Rome,
> Content thyself to be obscurely good.
> —Addison, *Cato* 4.4

THE PROBLEM of Washington's heroism can be looked at as an artist's quandary. It is the problem of neoclassical political art in general. How does one dramatize simplicity? How give stature to a *common* dignity? How single out what has been shared with all? "All men are created equal" was a hard creed for the artist, who was forced to be reductionist.

Jacques-Louis David's approach was to reduce all family members to a single denominator, citizenship. In his *Horatii,* the citizen prevails over the brother; in his *Brutus,* over the father. It is a code that can encourage ruthlessness. Having killed his sister, Horatius moves partway from citizen to *condottiere.* He will, in the person of Napoleon, become an heir to Hannibal (Plate 2). The problem of simplicity has not been solved but deferred, with a possibility of boomeranging, turning citizens into equal-opportunity tyrants. How does one strip away social distinctions without becoming brutal?

Benjamin West acquired his great Enlightenment reputation, one that seems exaggerated now, because he saw so clearly and so early what was required of revolutionary art. His achievement has been posed in partial and misleading terms, as a triumph of modern dress over classical garb. But fidelity to modern garb would not have moved men without other reductions. West stripped away baroque gesture—most notably in his *Agrippina* (Figure 71), where the billowy limbs and three-dimensionality of the arriving boat-

71   Benjamin West, *Agrippina with the Ashes of Germanicus* (1768)
. . . gestureless grief

men yield to the flat classical frieze of gestureless grief at the center. He gave up overt allegory and apotheosis. No emblem-book heroics define the "miracle" of Penn's peacemaking (Figure 66), no classical attributes define the roles of the peace ambassadors (Figure 65), no Britannia welcomes General Wolfe's sacrifice (Figure 53). In the *Death of General Wolfe,* the gestures toward victory at the city walls are like the boatmen's strain of limbs in the *Agrippina:* they define by contrast the intensity of real feeling in those who mourn motionless with the Indian.

Pursued far enough, West's reductionist approach would become a kind of eighteenth-century minimalism, seen for instance in Stuart's Vaughan and Athenaeum portraits (Figure 28). The work itself does not tell us that this is a President, a general, a hero. He is just a citizen. Then why were these particular features singled out from the citizenry at large for individual tracing? The answer, of course, is extra-aesthetic in this case. Washington's features were familiar enough by the 1790s to trigger emotion just by careful reproduction. Stuart was the beneficiary of established responses, which these works did not elicit on their own.

Absolute plainness is not obviously heroic. This is the difficulty that would dog so many representations of Washington, pushing them now toward grandiosity with Greenough, now toward triviality with McGuffey. Mere reduction belies the assertion of heroism. The apparent plainness that succeeded was actually using—subtly, almost subliminally—icons from the past, but ones recast in a fundamental way. West's *Death of General Wolfe* moved men by the pathos of a *concealed* pietà and the grandeur of a *suggested* classicism (in the Belvedere torso of the Indian). It was "modern" not because it denied the past but because it subordinated that past to new values. The same is true of Joseph Wright's secular nativity, or David's secular Pentecost. More common, of course, than Christian themes were disguised classical ones. West did not invent modern dress for heroic deaths, but he made a strong case for that choice. Nonetheless, the realistic modern figures are constantly taking their pose from the Apollo Belvedere (like Stuart's skater) or the dying gladiator (like Copley's Watson). Reduction did not mean a denial of reference, but a subordination of it, a forswearing of the overt symbol. Heroism persisted into the modern world, but only if it would submit to a new discipline, only if it shed the trappings of its old, aristocratic setting.

No one grappled in a more sustained way than Houdon with the problem of achieving simplicity without becoming, simply, dull. Even when Houdon draped Voltaire in a modern toga, he labored successfully to keep his chair from becoming a throne. Ingres painted a *statue* of the seated Napoleon (Figure 18); Houdon makes his sculpted Voltaire stir in the chair with conversational vitality and intimacy. In his simple busts, Houdon could suggest the soldier (Figure 35) or the ruler (Figure 37) by a minimal touch of attributes: the sword belt, the fillet. His bust of Franklin has a suggestion of chlamys, but it achieves its grandeur by a combination of photographic fidelity with ideality that owes nothing to classical stylization. (The Caffiéri bust of Franklin is a perfect contrast with Houdon's in this respect, and stands in the same relation to it as Greenough's head of Washington does to its Houdon model.)

Houdon's masterpiece for the combination of modern simplicity with republican grandeur is his statue of Washington. He was prepared to risk a great deal for the celebration of Washington's heroism, a great deal of his time and effort at the peak of his career. He took three assistants with him to America, and spent seventeen days at Mount Vernon modeling from his cast, measuring limbs, drawing sketches, watching the motions and expressions of his subject, making himself familiar with Washington's every physical aspect. He had consulted Franklin and Jefferson before making the trip. In America he talked about the work with

Charles Willson Peale and other Philadelphia artists. On his way through London, he visited the American art center in Benjamin West's studio and discussed his project with the great reformer. Washington's own opinions were enlisted. After Houdon's return to Paris, Jefferson considered the models Houdon worked on, and Gouverneur Morris struck poses imitative of Washington's. Houdon labored at the statue for a decade, and made over half a dozen busts considering various facets of the man. No one was better qualified to create a work adequate to Washington's greatness; to lift Washington to his proper level without enskying him away from us (like Greenough); yet to make him walk the common earth without diminishment.

The first decision was made, in accord with Virginia's commission, before Houdon left Paris. The work would not be colossal, but (in Jefferson's words) "the size shall be precisely that of life." Jefferson wrote to Benjamin Harrison, the governor of Virginia, that Houdon had agreed "to go to America to take the true figure by actual inspection and mensuration," so that there "might be a true evidence of his figure to posterity." No other treatment of Washington would be based on such thorough study of the living model, not even the portraits Trumbull based on the marathon sittings of 1790 (*Diaries* 6.30–51, 86–94).

But mere fidelity to the individual features, a kind of Vaughan portrait in stone, was out of the question. The effort and expense of worked marble demands justification in its own terms. The solemnity of the means leaves no room for ambiguity about the worthiness of the subject. Yet that solemnity cannot be asserted in too broad a way, where the subject is republican, without betraying the very ideal proposed.

The first choices were not hard, given Houdon's record. Life-size, not colossal—Houdon had done large-scale church sculpture (his St. John the Baptist and St. Bruno), but he preferred life scale

72   Enrico Causici, *Statue for Baltimore Monument* (1828)
. . . handing the commission into air

for his classic figures. Fidelity of portraiture, not stylization—that, too, was his general practice. Modern dress needed more consideration, which it received on both sides of the Atlantic. Full classical dress had been rejected by the time Houdon returned to Paris; but some compromise was still being considered when he made a model with ambiguous robe-toga (like that used in both his full statues of Voltaire). The reduction process continued as a classical pose was rejected. The only pose would be Washington's veritable posture. The Virginian's actual bearing was impressive; he would stand exactly as Houdon had observed him.

So far reduction. What of assertion? What positive statement could be made? What symbols or attributes would be admitted? In one model, Houdon joined to cloak and sandals the classical apparatus of fasces, Phrygian cap, and the plow of Cincinnatus. The other model seems to have used no symbol but a column, on which Washington hangs his sword. In the finished work, Houdon gracefully joined under Washington's left hand four attributes, two with a classical reference, all of which could be found as part of the furniture of Washington's world. In that sense, realism is not overtly abandoned. The symbolism comes from symbols met with in actual surroundings of the time.

What of theatrical "business"? What should Washington be doing? Here Houdon came up with a brilliant solution to the problem Canova (Figure 22) could meet only by borrowing from his own Perseus statue and by filling a classical scene with some distractingly literal modern "documentation" (the inscribed opening to the Farewell Address). Enrico Causici, too, sculpted Washington's surrender of power (Figure 72) for the Monument in Baltimore. He made Washington, on a high column, hand his commission out to the open air. The statue is a figure snatched from the tableau of Trumbull (Figure 5), where there are congressional officers to receive the document, and swept into the sky, where Washington's act is deprived of its context. I lived in Balti-

223

73   Roman copy, *Cincinnatus*
    . . . erring feet and hands

more for two decades and never found anyone who knew what Washington was *doing* up on that column.

But how *does* one dramatize in a single sculpted figure a scene like Trumbull's *Resignation,* with its extended *dramatis personae?* More to the point, how portray a complex sequence in one calm pose? Houdon handles this by showing, not the moment of Washington's resignation, but of his arrival back at Mount Vernon (Plate 6). He catches his subject in midtransformation from soldier to Virginia planter. Though Washington still wears his uniform, he has cast off his riding cloak, removed his sword, and taken up his walking stick. We witness a kind of spiritual "striptease" in which the emblems of power are being removed, one by one. Washington rests in the first moment of his return, at ease in the world he has chosen. No other actors are needed to complete the drama. He has reached his farm, and looks around at it. This is a secular and republican version of the Christian "removal" of dignities and offices celebrated by George Herbert:

> He did descend, undressing all the way.
> The starres His 'tire of light and rings obtain'd,
>   The cloud His bowe, the fire His spear,
>   The sky his azure mantle gain'd;
>   And when they ask'd what He would wear,
>   He smil'd, and said as He did go,
> He had new clothes a-making here below (*The Bag*).

Houdon may have arrived at the "stripping away" conception of this statue with help from the fact that the antique work known to the Enlightenment as "Cincinnatus" presented a man thought to be either loosing his sandal on returning home or binding it to leave his farm (Figure 73). In any case, as Herbert's incarnated God proves his greatness by setting it aside, so Houdon's Washington is reincarnated in his role and place as a domestic, agricultural figure. He towers as a citizen because he refuses to dominate as a soldier.

Thus the main "props" of the action are Washington's own clothing and stance, but each of the attributes added to the scene is important and brilliantly deployed. To take them one at a time—

1. The sword. In Canova's statue (Figure 22), Washington renounced his sword by placing it on the ground. Here he hangs it on the fasces, putting it at the disposal of the republic as he returns to the plow. The fasces is the axial norm between sword and plow, war and peace, as those exist in the life of a citizen, each to be taken up only as the common good requires. The sword's return is therefore provisional, but not upon Washington's will. Cincinnatus may be summoned out again, but that is not within his power to decide. The sword is for service, and must wait upon the call. David's second version of the *Horatii* also linked swords and plow, as the alternating service of patriots (Figure 12). But David stressed the *giving* of the swords, and threw the plow in shadow. Houdon's work implies that giving *up* the sword can be the higher, nobler task. No one better taught than Washington that the sword is readiest for its proper use when most swiftly relinquished after the crisis is over. He never glorified the sword. His own scheme of ornamentation at Mount Vernon was peaceful and rustic—he directed that a dove of peace, with the olive in its mouth, be used as weather vane. The cornice of the formal ballroom is decorated with harvest instruments. People who tried to make him talk about his war experiences were almost always disappointed (Freeman 6.35, 57). Charles Willson Peale, for whose military poses Washington sat, said, "What I have often admired in him is that he always avoided saying anything of the actions in which he was engaged in the last war" (ibid. 3.444). Gilbert Stuart found his subject equally unresponsive, until the subject of horses and farms came up. Washington lived by his words on taking up command:

I shall constantly bear in mind that as the sword was the last resort for the preservation of our liberties, so it ought to be the first to be laid aside when those liberties are firmly established (GW 6.464).

Houdon's sculpted first attribute gives us a simple eloquence of the sword surrendered.

2. The cloak. Somehow Washington's bulky military cloak became a standard part of the iconography of Washington's resignation. Perhaps Charles Willson Peale used it in his painting of Washington's return to the plow for his 1783 triumphal arch in Philadelphia. Causici wraps the cloak around Washington to give the suggestion of a toga (Figure 72). Trumbull shows it flung on a chair to indicate the speed of Washington's ride and arrival in Annapolis (Figure 5). The garment flung aside gives us a touch of willed drama, to prove the resignation is not a merely passive submission but an eager *assertion* of loyalty. So, in Houdon's work, the billowy contours of the cloak are contrasted, in front, with the tight symmetry of the fasces. At the back of the statue, the billows are counterpointed against the exquisite abstract pattern of pleats in Washington's coat. The disorderly tumble of the cloak suggests the stormy time Washington has lived through on the way back to domestic peace. But that storm *has* been ridden out. The cloak is thrown off.

3. The fasces. America was the first "fascist" country of the modern world—the first, that is, to make wide use of this symbol of a revived Roman republic. The French revolutionaries enthusiastically followed suit—the relationship of Washington to the fasces in Houdon's statue partly resembles that of David's design for Hercules standing by a fasces in the fourth stop of the Procession for the Festival of Brotherhood in 1793. The fasces were everywhere in early American art; and they are still encountered all over Washington—on bridges, on Lincoln's chair in his Monument, on the frames that hold Trumbull's paintings in the Rotunda. Columbia holds the fasces in Fragonard's depiction of Franklin (Fig-

ure 24). The table legs in Stuart's Lansdowne portrait are tapering fasces (Plate 5). William Rush's stern carving for the ship *Revolution* showed "the Genius of America binding the fasces with her right hand" (Bantel 12). Perhaps the largest pre-Mussolini fasces were raised to the heroes of Fort McHenry by Maximilian Godefroy (Figure 74).

The republic's binding of the disciplinary rods indicated the restraint on power used when citizens agree to obey laws of their own making. This is a particularly apt symbol for Washington, who felt that all real power is based on opinion, and who is shown by Houdon rejoining his fellow citizens. Houdon has added a humane Enlightenment touch to the fasces' sign of severity restrained—he bound into them Indian arrows, in the spirit of Penn's Treaty as painted by West. All mankind should live together as brothers on the American continent.

4. The plow. When historians discuss the ideal of agricultural virtue, they tend to associate it with Thomas Jefferson—or, sometimes, with James Madison; later on, with John Taylor of Caroline. Or they take it as an ideological mark of the "country" school of opposition to "court" influence and luxury. But, for his contemporaries, Washington was the obvious example of the virtuous farmer. And the cult of the plow as an instrument and symbol of virtue belonged to no single school in the Enlightenment. In France, this cult was to be met with outside the polemics of the physiocrats. In America, it was not the monopoly of the South. Much of it, in fact, came from the kind of classical education received at Harvard or Yale. It was part of the rhetorical tradition that glorified "the great Censor," the first Cato, who "toiled with his own hands." James Wilson developed this theme in his essay *On Property,* paraphrasing Cicero's *Pro Roscio Amerino* (18):

The wise and virtuous Numa was the patron of agriculture. He distributed the Romans into pagi or villages, and over each placed a superin-

74   Maximilian Godefroy, *Monument to Battle of Baltimore* (1815)
. . . pre-Mussolini fasces

tendant to prevail with them, by every motive, to improve the practice of husbandry. To inspire their industry with redoubled vigour, he frequently condescended to be their overseer himself. This wise and judicious policy had a most happy influence upon the subsequent manners and fortunes of Rome. Our consuls, said the Roman Orator, were called from the plough. Those illustrious characters, who have most adorned the commonwealth, and have been best qualified to manage the reins of government with dignity and success, dedicated a part of their time and of their labour to the cultivation of their landed estates. In those glorious ages of the republick, the farmer, the judge, and the soldier were to each other a reciprocal ornament. After having finished the publick business with glory and advantage to himself and to his country, the Roman magistrate descended, with modest dignity, from the elevation of the office; and reassumed, with contentment and with pleasure, the peaceful labours of a rural and independent life (McCloskey ed. 716).

Other Roman myths were revived, along with that of Cincinnatus, to glorify agriculture in the eighteenth century. Nicholas-Guy Brenet painted the huge draft animals that bring a plow into

75 Nicholas-Guy Brenet, *Gaius Furius Cressinus Accused of Sorcery* (1777)
. . . *Voici mes sortilèges*

the forum so that Gaius Furius Cressinus can refute the charge of
gaining wealth by sorcery (Figure 75): *"Voici mes sortilèges,"* he tells
his judges, with a gesture toward the source of all wealth. In the
year of Washington's Farewell Address, François-André Vincent
exhibited his *Agriculture,* in which a man brings his slippered and
delicate son to learn from a rough instructor where true values lie
(Figure 76). The instructor's literally shaping role is suggested by
the fact that Vincent gives him Michelangelo's arm of the Creator
from the Sistine ceiling. Greuze, in his painting at Moscow's Push-
kin Museum, shows the father passing on the plow to his son.

76 François-André Vincent, *Agriculture* (1796)
. . . the creating arm "makes a man" of the boy

In his Procession for the Festival of Brotherhood in 1793, David designed "a truly triumphal chariot consisting of a simple plow on which will be seated two old people, husband and wife; it will be drawn by their children, thus affording a touching example of filial piety and veneration for the aged." In America, the cult of agriculture was just as liturgically formal. In New York's 1788 parade to celebrate the ratification of the Constitution, there was "a new invented threshing machine conducted by Baron Pollnitz and other gentlemen in farmers' dresses, grinding and threshing grain" (*Diaries* 6.13).

No one was more responsive than Washington to the literal and symbolic appeal of the land. The most formal room at Mount Vernon—the equivalent of Jefferson's parlor, with its celebration of European arts and science—has nothing but agricultural ornament on cornice, lintels, and mantle. Farming technique was Washington's principal intellectual discipline, his favorite topic of conversation, the focus of his private correspondence. The bent of his mind was revealed when, during a break in the 1787 sessions of the drafting convention in Philadelphia, he rode out through the scenes of his old war activity. Here is the entire diary entry for August 31, 1787:

Tuesday 31st. Whilst Mr. Morris was fishing I rid over the old Cantonment [Valley Forge] of the American [force] of the Winter 1777, and 8. Visited all the Works, wch. were in Ruins; and the Incampments in woods where the ground had not been cultivated.

On my return back to Mrs. Moores, observing some Farmers at Work, and entering into Conversation with them, I received the following information with respect to the mode of cultivating Buck Wheat, and the application of the grain. Viz.—The usual time of sowing, is from the 10th. to the 20th. of July—on two plowings and as many harrowings at least—The grain to be harrowed in. That it is considered as an uncertain Crop being subject to injury by a hot sun whilst it is in blossom and quickly destroyed by frost, in Autumn—and that 25 bushls. is estimated as an average Crop to the Acre. That it is considered as an excellent food for horses, to puff and give them their *first* fat—Milch cattle, Sheep, and

Hogs and also for fatting Beeves. To do which, 2 quarts of Buck Wheat Meal, & half a peck of Irish Potatoes at the commencemt. (to be reduced as the appetite of the beasts decrease or in other words as they encrease in flesh) mixed and givn. 3 times a day is fully competent. That Buck wheat meal made into a wash is most excellent to lay on fat upon hogs but it must be hardened by feeding them sometime afterwards with Corn. And that this meal & Potatoes mixed is very good for Colts that are weaning. About 3 pecks of Seed is the usuall allowance for an Acre.

On my return to Mrs. Moores I found Mr. Robt. Morris & his lady there (*Diaries* 5.179).

Washington corresponded with England's leading agricultural theorist, Arthur Young. His friends knew that the way to please him was to send him new seeds, or cuttings, or animal breeds. In the period between the war and his presidency, he normally rode to all five of his farms and personally directed activities at each. His record was kept to compare each year's progress and problems with the preceding ones. A typical (if short) entry from 1787 runs:

Rid to all the Plantations & to the Ditchers. In the Neck set the best plowman (Nat) to marking Field No. 3 in 5 feet rows for Corn, Potatoes, Pease &ca. and finding the plow in No. 2 wet & heavy I directed the plows to list after Nat every alternate row as soon as he had got sufficiently ahead and in the meantime while No. 2 (which was in Corn last year) remained so wet to endeavour to plow the New field about to be taken in for Corn next year. Plowing and other work going on as usual at the other places. Began to Maul Rails for French's & to fit up two plows for plowing there (5.94).

When the weather was good, Washington would even take visitors with him on his rounds rather than let their arrival interfere with his close attention to detail (ibid. 100). His interest in growing things was aesthetic as well as economic, and he loved the gardens he laid out around the great house: "To see plants rise from the earth and flourish by the superior skill and bounty of the laborer fills a contemplative mind with ideas which are more easy to be conceived than expressed" (GW 29.205). His belief in the joys of rural life equaled that of any physiocrat. As he wrote Lafayette:

"The tumultuous populace of large cities are ever to be dreaded. Their indiscriminate violence prostrates for the time all public authority and its consequences are sometimes extensive and terrible."

There was one horrible blot on this idyllic world of the southern farmer: slaves. Washington increasingly felt the horror. At the war's end, he discouraged his fellow Virginians from their effort to regain slaves freed by the British (GW 26.364, 370, 401–2, 405–8)—which indicates that he sided with the abolitionist Hamilton against Jefferson when the latter was insisting on reparation for lost slaves as part of the treaty with England. As President, Washington was sensitive to the scandal of a national leader holding slaves, and he hired white servants to do the publicly visible work at his residence (Flexner 4.124). During the war, he had consulted with Lafayette on plans for manumitting slaves to a free island (ibid. 118–19). As time went by, he considered other schemes. One problem in tracing his thought on this matter is that he had to keep it secret from his neighbors (ibid. 125). For one thing, simply to amass the fund needed, for care of freed slaves unable to work or to find work, he would have to maintain the value of his land and the price of his crops, which would be endangered if other Virginians knew what he was up to. It will be remembered that Jefferson delayed as long as he could the publication of his *Notes on the State of Virginia* because he anticipated the opposition of his countryman to its proposal for sending emancipated slaves to free territory. It was with a view to their manumission that Washington endeavored to keep black families intact (ibid. 441–42) and to develop marketable skills in them (all five of his farms had black overseers by the time Washington assumed the presidency, ibid. 436). Despite many difficulties, Washington collected the fund needed to free all his own slaves at Martha's death (ibid. 445–47). The last payments were made from that fund in 1833—though not according to Washington's will. He had provided for the education of the freedmen's children, against which the state of Virginia passed a law after his death. Slavery irrevocably taints all those involved in its train of evil consequences, as Washington knew. But the fact remains that he was the only founder of this nation who managed to free his slaves. It was the last and greatest debt he owed to his own honor.

For the relationship of the Houdon statue's four attributes to the figure of Washington himself, the sculptor took advantage of the peculiarity of his subject's stance. Washington was very tall, strong, and well coordinated, as graceful at dancing as at horsemanship. But his body was oddly put together. He had a protruding rib cage, sloping shoulders, long arms, and very large hands— large enough, his step-grandson said, to embarrass him. If Washington had let himself slouch at all, he would have looked like an ape, about to scrape the backs of his knuckles along the ground. Part of the air of discipline that he exuded came from the fact that he adopted a compensatorily erect carriage, one so upright that it is frequently mentioned as a distinguishing mark. He carried his head so high and "tucked in" that he seemed almost to lean backward. Christian Gullager, the Danish artist whose limited technique did not prevent him from catching tricks of expression or individuality in most of his portraits, concentrated on the characteristic cock of Washington's head, which helped form the dewlap that shows in most portraits of him, though William Maclay and others thought Washington thin during his presidential years (Figure 77). In the very first painting ever made of Washington, Charles Willson Peale's of 1772 (Figure 31), we see the veteran of the French and Indian War drawing himself up above the painter (and, incidentally, hiding his hands)—though the pose is derived, in part, from Joshua Reynolds' portrait of Thomas Needham.

Houdon uses Washington's characteristic stance to give his work its shifting vitality as one moves about it. By the lofty carriage of his head, the sculpted figure can stand *by* the fasces with his head *behind* them—he tapers from us as we come at him, just like his Monument. This plays optical tricks on the angle of the

77   Christian Gullager, *George Washington*
. . . the characteristic cock of the head

fasces, which seem out of plumb, but which also seem to tilt in *different* directions when seen from different angles. Into the interplay of such lines Houdon introduces the canted sword, the swooping lines of the plow, the balancing of the slim walking stick over against the clustered attributes. Though Washington is at ease, there is a kinetic realigning of the verticals whenever one moves this way or that in his presence. It is a statue with ambulatory angles, despite its serenity. Houdon's careful tilting of his lines can be seen in the way he elongates Washington's left thigh to get just the interplay he wants with other slopes and tilts.

Houdon could, when he wanted to, mold forms as fluid and self-enclosed as a Brancusi (see *La Frileuse,* Figure 78). But here he has aerated his stone. The heroism is in the technique, creating large Virginia farm space under the right arm, which is propped on the slim walking stick—all fashioned from one piece of Italian marble. The "opening out" is done with a classical restraint that should be measured against the Renaissance approach to a body's interplay with an angled stick: the *St. Longinus* of Bernini, a disciplined explosion of emotion, flowing and free, yet complexly triangulated in structure (Figure 79). Bernini is presenting a conversion event—from soldier to Christian—in the most dramatic way he could. Here man is visibly remade by the impact of grace. Houdon's hero converts himself—from soldier to farmer—by an interior strength that is as calm as it is purposive. The features are not twisted but settled, a Roman mask, moving in its very impassivity, made more tender by the effort at severity. And where Bernini puts Longinus in a niche, to be seen from only one side and in a predetermined light, Houdon puts Washington out in our common air, a citizen among citizens.

The Virginians have made a great mistake in putting the statue high on a pedestal. This gives viewers a weirdly intimate introduction to Washington's shoe manufactory, but makes the play of light across his face impossible to see with clarity. Washington should touch down on his native earth—or at least on the floor of the Roman temple designed by Jefferson. When the Baltimore Art Museum put together its Bicentennial exhibit, it devoted one room to Houdon busts. The others were put along the walls or in the corners, but Washington's head was placed in the center of the room, at the height it would have been if we had met Washington at Mount Vernon. It was eerie to turn a corner and see those eyes staring past the heads and shoulders of the viewers who moved

78   Jean-Antoine Houdon, *La Frileuse* (1781–83)
. . . liquid and enclosed as a Brancusi

79   Gianlorenzo Bernini, *St. Longinus* (1629–38)
. . . conversion as an explosion of emotion

around him. The effect the Richmond statue would make at its proper height can be seen even from the crude metal cast of the statue that stands on the museum floor at the Chicago Art Institute. Washington continues to elude us; but Houdon comes close to making him walk back among us, heroic but not distant after all. The statue is enough to make one remember the last part of Henry Lee's famous sentence about him, the part that is most often omitted but which gives its real force to the famous anaphora of the opening: "First in war, first in peace, first in the hearts of his countrymen, he was second to none in the humble and endearing scenes of private life" (*Eulogies* 17).

It has been said that Washington was the last of the classical heroes, as Napoleon was the first of the romantic heroes. But that is not the impression one gets by comparing Houdon's statue with, say, Canova's *Napoleon* (Figure 19). The contrast is not so much between two eras as between two conceptions of the morality of power. And it was, after all, a romantic poet, Lord Byron, who ended his *Ode to Napoleon* this way:

> There was a day—there was an hour,
>   While earth was Gaul's—Gaul thine—
> When that immeasurable power
>   Unsated to resign
> Had been an act of purer fame
> Than gathers round Marengo's name,
>   And gilded thy decline
> Through the long twilight of all time,
> Despite some passing clouds of crime.
>
> But thou forsooth must be a king,
>   And don the purple vest
> As if that foolish robe could wring
>   Remembrance from thy breast.
> Where is that faded garment? where
> The gewgaws thou wert fond to wear,
>   The star—the string—the crest?
> Vain froward child of empire! say,
> Are all thy playthings snatch'd away?

Where may the wearied eye repose
    When gazing on the Great;
Where neither guilty glory glows,
    Nor despicable state?
Yes—one—the first—the last—the best:
The Cincinnatus of the West
    Whom envy dared not hate,
Bequeath'd the name of Washington
To make men blush there was but one.

KEY TO BRIEF CITATIONS

Baker   W. S. Baker. *Character Portraits of Washington as Delivered by Historians, Orators, and Divines.* Philadelphia, 1837.

Bantel   Linda Bantel *et al. William Rush, American Sculptor.* Pennsylvania Academy of Fine Arts, 1982.

Bryan   William Alfred Bryan. *George Washington in American Literature, 1775–1865.* Columbia University Press, 1952.

Chinard   Gilbert Chinard. *George Washington as the French Knew Him.* Princeton, 1940.

Diaries   *The Diaries of George Washington.* Edited by Donald Jackson and Dorothy Twohig. Vols. I–VI. University of Virginia, 1976–79.

Eulogies   *Eulogies and Orations on the Life and Death of George Washington.* Boston, 1800.

Farrand   Max Farrand. *The Records of the Federal Convention of 1787,* revised edition. Vols. I–IV. Yale, 1966.

Flexner   James Thomas Flexner. *George Washington.* Vols. I–IV. Little, Brown, 1965–72.

Freeman   Douglas Southall Freeman. *George Washington.* Vols. I–VII. Scribner's, 1948–57.

GW   *The Writings of George Washington.* Edited by John C. Fitzpatrick. Thirty-nine volumes. Washington, 1931–44.

Honour	Hugh Honour. *Neoclassicism*. Penguin, 1968.
JWCI	*Journal of the Warburg and Courtauld Institutes.*
Marshall	John Marshall. *The Life of Washington*. Vols. I–V. Philadelphia, 1805.
McGroarty	William Buckner McGroarty. *Washington: First in the Hearts of His Countrymen: Orations by Men Who Had Known Washington.* Richmond, 1932.
Paltsits	Victor Hugo Paltsits. *Washington's Farewell Address.* New York, 1935.
Praz	Mario Praz. *Conversation Pieces*. Pennsylvania State, 1971.
Royster	Charles Royster. *A Revolutionary People at War: The Continental Army and American Character, 1775–1783.* Chapel Hill: University of North Carolina at Chapel Hill Press, 1979.
Seznec	Jean Seznec. *Essais sur Diderot et l'Antiquité.* Oxford, 1957.
Silverman	Kenneth Silverman. *A Cultural History of the American Revolution.* Crowell, 1976.
Starobinski	Jean Starobinski. *1789, The Emblems of Reason*, translated by Barbara Bray. University of Virginia, 1982.
WMQ	*William and Mary Quarterly.*

BIBLIOGRAPHICAL ESSAY

BIOGRAPHIES OF WASHINGTON

IF WE HAVE trouble understanding Washington, we must blame the historical changes that separate us from him, not the biographers, who have served him well. John Marshall (1804–7) and Washington Irving (1855–59) set high scholarly standards for their day. And, hard as that is to imagine now, so did Washington's editors, Jared Sparks (1834–37), and Worthington Chauncey Ford (1889–93). Ford's edition was undertaken to mark the one hundred and fiftieth anniversary of Washington's birth, which also occasioned a serviceable biography by Henry Cabot Lodge (1889) and a silly one by Woodrow Wilson (1896).

The golden age of Washington studies was initiated in 1932, the bicentennial of his birth, which occasioned the life by John C. Fitzpatrick (1933) and the unfinished (and mildly iconoclastic) one by Rupert Hughes (1926–30). More important, the anniversary prompted the most complete edition of Washington's writings to this day, by John C. Fitzpatrick (1931–44). The ground was thus prepared for the best biography of Washington, surely one of the best military and political biographies ever produced in America, that of Douglas Southall Freeman (1948–54, final volume completed by Freeman's assistants in 1957). Freeman has to be corrected by some later findings—he takes more seriously than recent scholars the reality of a "Conway Cabal"—but he is less the advocate of Washington than are most biographers who have lived with their subjects for years. Freeman admits Washington's intellectual limits and military blunders. In fact, he sometimes blames him where a case can be made for Washington's conduct; e.g., his reluctance to reenter political life in 1787 (6.84–86). The limitation that Dumas Malone singled out (in a fine appreciation of Freeman contained in Vol. 6), that Freeman resolutely served by Washington's side, year by year, not allowing for later events, confining himself as much as possible to Washington's purview at each moment, gives vitality to his extraordinarily detailed picture. Freeman actually does what Washington Irving boasted he was doing in the 1850s:

I had a great deal of trouble to keep the different parts together, giving a little touch here and a little touch there, so that one part should not lag behind the other nor one part be more conspicuous than the other. I felt like old Lablache when he was performing in a rehearsal of his orchestra . . . bringing out a violin here, a clarinet there, now suppressing a trombone, now calling upon the flutes, and every now and then bringing out the big bass drum.

Freeman's artistry, not to be discerned in the one-volume condensation done by another, rested on the elaborate outlining he did for each chapter. Malone quotes a diary entry of March 13, 1947: "Finished outline of Chapter XVII ["Braddock's Defeat"]. It took about 11 hours and will save 20 at least" (6.xxvi). Typical of his methods was the division of labor for Chapter VIII ["Washington at Fort Le Boeuf"]: twenty-five hours of outlining, forty-two hours of composing, and seventeen hours of revision. The impact of such thorough organization and clear sifting of relevant factors is cumulative, but reaches a great intensity, at, for instance, 4.325–46, pages that trace almost hour by hour the considerations, anxieties, and obstacles that crowded in on Washington as he had to decide what risks to take, if any, in following up his victory at Trenton. The blend of action and risk, hesitation and daring, that Washington displayed at this juncture, the way he had to *create* his army, even in victory, at the very edge of defeat, is conveyed in a way that no shorter narrative could ever accomplish. The result is detailed but shapely, deploying large forces with scholarly generalship.

Freeman's style was formed on nineteenth-century models, but he has a solid and formal eloquence that does justice to the dignity of his subject without becoming dull. No one could speak with better authority about all the factors that must go into an estimate of Washington: "Knox or Jonathan Trumbull, Jr., or David Humphreys, or almost any other of those who remained with him to the end might have taken him apart, quality by quality, but they could not easily have put him back together again" (5.496). Freeman comes as close as anyone is likely to.

On Freeman's achievement all later studies of Washington have been built—for instance, James Thomas Flexner's sprightly four-volume biography (1965–72), which adds some material made available since Freeman's time, especially on Washington's slaves. Marcus Cunliffe's 1958 biographical essay, *George Washington: Man and Monument,* was my own introduction to the subject, and in its 1982 revision (Mentor) it remains, I think, the best introduction. Edmund Morgan's *The Genius of George Washington* (Norton, 1980), combines a brilliant lecture with a superb anthology of passages from Washington's correspondence. For Washington's military tasks and leadership, Charles Royster is excellent in *A Revolutionary People at War* (North Carolina, 1979). So is Robert Middlekauff, *The Glorious Cause* (Oxford, 1982).

I

FROM NEWBURGH TO ANNAPOLIS

For the Newburgh mutiny, see Richard H. Kohn, "The Inside Story of the Newburgh Conspiracy," WMQ 1970, pp. 187–220, also 1972, pp. 151–58; and Paul David Nelson, "Horatio Gates at Newburgh, 1783," ibid. 1972, pp. 143–51.

For Trumbull's resignation picture in the Rotunda, see Jules David Prown in *John Trumbull, the Hand and Spirit of a Painter* (by Helen Cooper et al., Yale, 1982), 89–90.

II
DICTATOR

For Washington's Enlightenment attitude toward religion, see Paul Boller, Jr., *George Washington and Religion* (Dallas, 1963). Freeman (2.388) notes that: "In no surviving letter of his [Washington's] youth is the name of Jesus used; 'Providence' appears more frequently than 'God.'" Jay Fliegelman adds that Washington's "twenty volumes of correspondence reveal not a single mention of Christ" (*Prodigals and Pilgrims,* Cambridge, 1982, p. 212).

III
WEEMS AND CINCINNATUS

For the comparison of Washington to Moses, see *Eulogies* 22, 36, 157, 171, 274; Baker 13, 16, 118; Bryan 59, 60, 63, 70, 73, 87, 112; Silverman 501–2. There is a good collection of texts in Robert Hay's article, "George Washington, American Moses," *American Quarterly* 1969, 780–91.

For the comparison of Washington to Joshua, see *Eulogies* 171; Baker 118; Catherine L. Albanese, *The Sons of the Fathers* (Temple, 1976), 154–55; and Kenneth Silverman, *Timothy Dwight* (Twayne, 1969), 24–36.

For Dwight's epic, see George Sensabaugh, *Milton in America* (Princeton, 1964), 166–76, and Silverman 500–3. For Barlow's epic, Sensabaugh 176–78 and Silverman 519–36.

For Washington as Cincinnatus, see *Eulogies* 17, 64, 165–66, 206; Baker 30, 120, 133, 375; Bryan 53, 77, 123, 167; Silverman 429–

30, 434. The comparison was a commonplace of July Fourth toasts and poems—e.g., in the New York *Daily Advertiser* of July 5, 1786:

> Great CINCINNATUS, first and best,
> Thy merits ne'er can be exprest,
>   Though every Muse attends.
> 'Twas thou alone, divinely taught,
> That strangely conquer'd, nobly fought,
>   Attended by thy friends.

For later uses of the Cincinnatus image, see M. E. Thistlethwaite, *The Image of George Washington* (University of Pennsylvania, 1977), 121–27. Only one classical type, Fabius, competed with Cincinnatus in defining Washington's heroism, and that one faded as Washington's achievements broadened beyond the military. But, as David Humphreys wrote in his *Poem on the Death of George Washington,*

> Long held th'accomplished Chief the Fabian name . . .

And Barlow's *Columbiad* has these lines:

> In vain sage Washington from hill to hill
> Plays round his foes with more than Fabian skill;
> Retreats, advances, lures them to his snare
> To balance numbers by the shifts of war (5.283–86).

For other references to Washington as Fabius, see *Eulogies* 64, 73, 113, 133, 171, 276; Baker 94, 118, 120, 144, 275; Bryan 61, 67, 77, 143; Chinard 20, 24, 31, 81, 84; McGroarty 61, 89, 118.

IV

WEEMS AND THE CHERRY TREE

For the letters of Weems, see the three volumes of Emily Ford Skeel's *Mason Locke Weems: His Works and Ways* (New York: 1929).

The travesty of Weems by the McGuffey Readers should be quoted in full (Eclectic Series, *New Third Reader,* Lesson LXXXIV, "George and the Hatchet"):

Never, perhaps did a parent take more pains, than did the father of General Washington, to fix in the mind of his son George an early love of *truth.*

"Truth, George," said he, "is the most lovely trait of youth. I would ride fifty miles, my son, to see the boy whose heart is so *honest* and whose lips so *pure,* that we may depend on *every word* he *says.*

"How lovely does such a child appear in the eyes of all! Parents will praise him before their children, and wish them to follow his example. They will often invite him to visit them, and when he comes, will receive him with *joy,* and treat him with the greatest favor.

"But, O George, how far from this is the case with the boy who is given to *lying!* Good people avoid him wherever he goes; and parents *dread* to see him in company with their children.

"O George, rather than see you come to this, dear as you are to me, *gladly* would I assist to nail you up in your little coffin, and follow you to your grave.

"Hard, indeed, it would be to me to give up my son, whose feet are always so ready to run about with me, and whose smiling face and sweet prattle make me so happy. But still I would give him up, rather than see him a common liar."

"Father," said George, with tears in his eyes, "do I ever tell lies?"

"No, George. I thank God you do *not,* my son; and I rejoice in the hope you *never will.* Whenever you do any thing wrong, which may often be the case, as you are but a little boy yet, you must never say what is not true, to conceal it, but come bravely up, my son, like a little *man,* and *tell* me of it."

When George was about six years old, he was made the owner of a little hatchet, with which he was much pleased, and went about chopping every thing that came in his way.

One day, when in the garden, he thoughtlessly tried the edge of his hatchet on a fine young English cherry-tree, which he cut so badly as to destroy it.

The next morning, the old gentleman, finding out what had happened to his favorite tree, came into the house, and with much warmth, asked who had done the mischief. Nobody could tell him anything about it. At this moment, George came in with his hatchet.

"George," said his father, "do you know who killed that fine cherry-tree yonder in the garden?"

This was a *hard question*. George was silent for a moment. Then, looking at his father, his young face bright with the love of truth, he bravely cried out, "I can't tell a *lie,* father. You *know* I can't tell a *lie. I* cut it with my hatchet."

"Come to my *arms,* my dearest boy!" cried his father; *"come* to my *arms!* you killed my cherry-tree, George, but you have now paid me for it a thousand-fold. *Such* proof of heroic truth in my son is of more value than a *thousand* trees, though they were all of the purest *gold."*

For some shrewd comments on Weems, see Jay Fliegelman, *Prodigals and Pilgrims* (Cambridge, 1982), 201–2.

V

GREENOUGH AND PHEIDIAS

For Greek concepts of "dexterity," see Geoffrey Lloyd, "Right and Left in Greek Philosophy" (*Journal of Hellenic Studies,* 1962), 55–66. One could add to his Greek citations others from Latin writers—e.g., Pliny's advice that the sower should, for best results, sow with the right hand (*Natural History* 18.24). Aristotle's ranking of the body's parts in terms of their nobility—giving precedence to the right, the top, and the front—gave a kind of hierarchy to all later considerations of the "little universe" of man. Plato thought that souls ascend in rightward spirals (*Republic* 614c16–21), a concept that should be compared with Singleton's description of Dante's climb, cited in my text.

For the Christian imagery of the right hand, which often applied Psalm 110.1 to Jesus, see the entries under "Right-Left" in Michael Darton's *Modern Concordance to the New Testament* (Doubleday, 1976), p. 485. Actually, Jesus is rarely shown at the Father's right hand in Christian art; but this reflects a sensitivity to the right-left symbolism, not a departure from it. Trinitarian doctrine had developed the notion of the Holy Spirit's equality to the other two Persons in God, and a right-hand position for Jesus would have consigned the Spirit to the less-preferred left side. So, in baptism and crucifixion scenes, the Trinity is shown with all persons in the center, Father at the top, Spirit descending, the Son incarnated on earth.

Some have argued that the viewer's left is the "strong" position in paintings because of our habit of reading from left to right—but that influence makes the viewer's *right* the emphatic one, as *climactic* (see John Shearman and John White on the order of Raphael's cartoons, *Art Bulletin* 40, 1958, pp. 194–221). Michael Fried notices the division of some eighteenth-century paintings into a male left and female right, but traces this to the influence of Poussin's *Testament of Eudamidas* (cf. *Theatricality and Absorption,* University of California, 1980, p. 193). Trumbull's division of his paintings into male and female sides may have been influenced by David's *Horatii,* which he saw and admired in David's studio in 1786, the same year that he completed his own *Death of General Montgomery* (Figure 55). Jules David Prown notes the similar composition of the two paintings—a pyramid formed by male limbs and weapons on the left; collapsing and mourning figures on the right—and concludes "It seems unlikely that two such similar compositional elements could have been arrived at simultaneously" (in Helen Cooper et al., *John Trumbull, the Hand and Spirit of a Painter,* Yale, 1982, p. 33). Yet Prown also admits that the paintings seem to have been completed before the two men met.

For Hauer's *Lafayette and Madame Roland,* see Paul L. Grigaut, *Art Quarterly,* 1951, 350–51.

For Ingres's use of Charlemagne imagery in his 1806 *Napoleon Enthroned,* see Susan Siegfried, *Proceedings of the Consortium on Revolutionary Europe* 2 (Athens, Georgia, 1980) 69–81.

For David's *Death of Socrates,* its precursors and successors, see Seznec 17–20, with Plates 2, 3, 5–9. The leg lifted onto the bed in David's 1787 painting, after being freed from its chains, may be derived from a 1774 sketch by Bernard Rode engraved in 1776 (Seznec Plate 5)—though Rode has Socrates rub his ankle to restore circulation! In this sketch, alone of the examples Seznec gives, Plato is at the foot of Socrates' bed, in profile, with his writing instruments. Another work of special interest is by Cignaroli, who presents Socrates' death as a pietà (Seznec Plate 2).

For Trumbull's *Washington at Verplanck's Point,* see the article by Edgar Richardson, *Winterthur Portfolio* III (1967) 1–23.

VI

NONALIGNMENT

For Edmund Morgan's discussion of the neutrality policy, see his George Rogers Clark lecture, *The Genius of George Washington* (Norton, 1980).

VII

CHARACTER

N. T. Phillipson discusses the "spectatorial" clubs in Edinburgh—which help explain the bond Franklin felt between his own efforts and Lord Kames's—in "Culture and Society in the Eighteenth-Century Province" (*The University in Society,* Vol. II, ed. L. Stone, Princeton, 1975) and in his forthcoming *The Origins of Scottish Civic Humanism.*

VIII

FAME

For the furnishings of Monticello, I rely on Jefferson's 1809 manuscript "Catalogue of Paintings, etc. at Monticello," quoted by permission of the Jefferson Papers, Tracy W. McGregor Library (#2958), University of Virginia. In the years after he drew up that catalogue, Jefferson continued to add American heroes to his shrine, including another tier of busts—information for which I am grateful to James A. Bear, Jr., Curator of the Thomas Jefferson Memorial Foundation at Monticello. At his Poplar Forest home, Jefferson had William Rush's bust of Washington (Estate Sale, Jan. 15, 1827). For the cult of Doric simplicity, see Honour, 126.

For Jefferson's insistence on precedent with Benjamin Latrobe, see *The Eye of Jefferson* (National Gallery of Art, 1976), 261–62. For the equation of antiquity with nature, see William Dunlap, *History of the Rise and Progress of the Arts of Design in the United States* (1834 edition in Dover reprint) 1.10; Honour 61, 106; Seznec 106.

For Ceracchi, the best treatment of his Washington bust is by Ulysse Desportes, "Giuseppe Ceracchi in America and His Busts of George Washington," *Art Quarterly* 1963, 141–78. The judgment of contemporaries who thought this the best likeness of Washington is discussed on pages 171–72. Desportes also notes that Ceracchi's bust of Jefferson (now lost) was preferred by Jefferson's family to that done by Houdon. For Ceracchi's bust of Napoleon, I am indebted to correspondence with Professor Desportes, who was also kind enough to show me his correspondence on the subject with Gérard Hubert.

For the Enlightenment's cult of antiquity, see *Classical Traditions in Early America,* edited by John Eadie (University of Michigan, 1976), especially the essay by James McLachlan, "Classical Names, American Identities." Also Harold Talbot Parker, *The Cult of Antiquity and the French Revolutionaries* (University of Chicago, 1937).

For the importance of Voltaire's *Brutus* in the French Revolution, see Robert L. Herbert, *Voltaire, "Brutus" and the French Revolution* (London, 1977), 71–112.

For classical pageantry, see David Lloyd Dowd, *Pageant-Master of the Republic: Jacques-Louis David* (University of Nebraska,

1948), 46–67. For Charles Willson Peale as the pageant-master of the American Revolution, see Silverman 425–26, 582–85.

For the conscious effort to institute a classical imagery in America, see Frank H. Sommer, "Thomas Hollis and the Arts of Dissent," in *Prints in and of America to 1850,* edited by John D. Morse (University of Virginia, 1970) and Clarence S. Brigham, *Paul Revere's Engravings* (New York, 1969), 26–31, 113–14.

For the importance of fame to the encouragement of virtue, see Douglass Adair's introduction to *The Spur of Fame* (Huntington Library, 1966) and the title essay in his *Fame and the Founding Fathers* (Norton, 1974). Also Royster 204–12, and Honour 83, 132, 153.

IX
ROLE

For the importance of Addison's *Cato* in America, see Frederic M. Litto, "Addison's *Cato* in the Colonies" (WMQ 1966); Meyer Reinhold, *The Classick Pages* (University of Pennsylvania, 1975), 147–51; Paul Leicester Ford, *Washington and the Theater* (New York, 1899), 1, 3, 26; and Samuel Eliot Morison, "The Young Washington," in *By Land and by Sea* (New York, 1953). For the comparison of Washington to Cato, see Baker 120, 126, 275; Bryan 179; McGroarty 104, 121; Silverman 430. For the influence of Addison's play on Voltaire, see Adolphe G. Hegnauer, *Der Einfluss von "Addison's Cato,"* Hamburg, 1912, 98–100. Two new plays about Cato were performed in Paris during the first year of the Revolution, 1789 (ibid. 102).

For the contrast between Washington and Caesar, see *Eulogies* 34, 64, 73, 84, 224, 241; Bryan 191; Chinard 88; Royster 261.

XI

SACRIFICE

For West's use of the deposition type, see Charles Mitchell, "Benjamin West's *Death of Wolfe* and the Popular History Piece" (JWCI 1944), 20–33. For the Enlightenment fascination with martyrs, see Seznec 11–12, paraphrasing Diderot: "Christianity, however false, has never lacked martyrs; how is enlightenment (*philosophie*) to conquer superstition if no philosophe is ready to profess the truth unto death as a hundred fanatics have done for a deception?" Compare Honour 146–59. For the comparison of secular and theological pietàs, Seznec (6–7) quotes Rousseau: "The death of Socrates, philosophizing calmly with his friends, is as sweet as one could want. That of Jesus, expiring in torments, mocked, derided, cursed by everyone, is as horrible as one could fear . . . Yes, if the life and death of Socrates are those of a wise man, the life and death of Jesus are those of a God." The cult of the political martyr in religious terms reached its climax in the six-hour funeral of Marat, at which a hymn was sung ("O coeur de Jésus, O coeur de Marat"). Later, Marat's heart was hung in an urn from the ceiling of the Cordeliers Club.

For William Rush's connection of sacrifice with the freed republic's eagle in his *Schuylkill Chained,* see his program for stern carvings on the ship *Constellation:*

The Constellation should be represented by an elegant female characteristic of indignant Nature, at the period of the American Revolution, determined on the forming of a New Creation, from that Chaos of Ignorance, vice and folly, which she had long been burdened with—She should have a flaming torch in her right hand, setting fire to the bursting World under her feet, with the emblems of Tyranny, Superstition, Folly etc. issuing from it, and thrown into Confusion and fermentation, her left arm resting on the altar of Liberty. The American eagle in the act of flight . . . (Bantel 13).

For the revolutionary content of David's *Horatii* (against a recent tendency to play that down), see Thomas Crow, *Art History* I, 1978, pages 424–71. For the Toledo museum's copy of the work, attributed to David in its catalogue, see R. Rosenblum, *Burlington Magazine* 1965, 473–75. Rosenblum claims that the copy was done by David's student Girodet, though David signed and dated it for a prominent patron and allowed a resale under his name. In any case, the work must have been done under his supervision.

XII

HEAD AND HEART

For references to Franklin as Prometheus, see Alfred Owen Aldridge, *Franklin and his French Contemporaries* (New York University, 1957), 66, 80, 106, 123–25, 196, 213. For Franklin as Nestor, ibid. 137, 194; as Mentor, 135.

For Joseph Wright's secular nativity, see Ronald Paulson, *Emblem and Expression* (Harvard, 1975), 190–91. For Diderot's attitude on the secularizing of religious imagery, see Seznec 113–14. Michelet, in his history of the French Revolution, wrote of the Tennis Court Oath: *"Ce fut comme la crèche pour la nouvelle religion, son étable de Bethlehem"* (Pleiade 110).

For West's Peace Commissioners, see Arthur S. Marks, "Benjamin West and the American Revolution," *American Art Journal* 1974, which also treats Trumbull's attempt to paint the scene (133–35).

XIII

THE ROUNDED IMAGE

For Houdon's masterpiece, see John S. Hallam, "Houdon's Richmond Statue of Washington," *American Art Journal* 1978, 73–80.

For the problem of republican simplicity in art, see Seznec,

100–1. For West's contribution to this movement, see Edgar Wind's seminal essay "The Revolution in History Paintings" (JWCI 1938–39), 116–27. For the question of classical nudity, see Honour 114–22.

For David's Hercules with his left arm on the fasces, see Antoine Schnapper, *David* (Alpine Fine Arts, 1982), 138.

For the statue known as "Cincinnatus" in the eighteenth century, see Francis Haskell and Nicholas Penny, *Taste and the Antique* (Yale, 1981), 182–84. An ancient copy of the work was owned by the Earl of Lansdowne, who commissioned Stuart's painting of the modern Cincinnatus in his presidential office.

INDEX

Page numbers in italics refer to illustrations

George Washington Giving the Laws
(anon.), 138, *139*
Gérard, Marguérite, *Eripuit Coelo,*
73, 74
See also Fragonard, Jean-Ho-
noré
Gesture, Washington's sense of,
104–5
Ghana in Transition (Apter), 20
Giotto, 215
Godefroy, Maximilian, *Monument*
to Battle of Baltimore, 228, *229*
Govan, Thomas, 138
Government
and consent of the governed, 101
and opinion, 99–100
Grasse, François-Joseph-Paul,
Comte de, 5, 94
Greco, El, 215
Greenough, Horatio, *George*
Washington, xxv, 53, 55, 67–68,
72, 74, 220
Gregory, John, *Comparative View*
of the State and Faculties of
Man with Those of the Animal
World, 51
Greuze, Jean-Baptiste, 231
Gros, Antoine-Jean, *Napoleon at*
Jaffa, 190, 190–91
Gullager, Christian, *George Wash-*
ington, 235, *236*
Gunpowder Plot, 30

Hale, Nathan, 29, 132, 134, 174
Hallam, John S., 118
Hamilton, Alexander, 24, 50, 96,
128, 189, 233
on Charles Lee, 31
on freedom of the press and
public opinion, 101
on popular opinion, 102

view on greatest man, 137–38
and Washington's foreign pol-
icy, 93, 94, 95
Washington's warning to, 6–7
Hancock, John, 24, 211, 213
Hand, left vs. right, significance
of, 55–67
Hanniel, 29, 31
Harrison, Benjamin, 5, 221
Hauer, Jean-Jacques, *Lafayette and*
Madame Roland, 59, 60–61
Hawthorne, Nathaniel, on
Greenough's *Washington,* 68
Henry, Patrick, 92, 132, 134
Herbert, George, 225
Hero factory, Houdon's atelier as,
117–18, 121
Heroic age, Jefferson and making
of, 110–17
Heroic models, shaping behavior
after, 126
Heroism of Washington, as art-
ist's quandary, 217–20
Hero worship, 109–10, 129–30
History, significance of chance in,
110
Houdon, Jean-Antoine, 14, 117–18,
220, 221
atelier as hero factory, 117–18, 121
The Emperor Napoleon, 120, *121,*
220
The Flayed Man, 117
La Frileuse, 237, *238*
George Washington (bust), 118,
119, 220
George Washington (full-length,
Richmond statue), *frontis.,*
color plate foll. p. 38, 118, 220–
21, 222–23, 225–28, 235–37, 240
Jefferson on, 128
plaster busts at Monticello, 112

Houdon in His Studio (Boilly), *114,*
117–18
Howard, Leon, 28
Hudibrastics (Brackenridge), 140
Hughes, Robert Ball, *John Trum-
bull,* 142, *143*
Hume, David, 101, 115, 122
on government and opinion, 99
*Inquiry Concerning the Princi-
ples of Morals,* 198
Of National Character, 102
Humphreys, David, 24, 140
on Washington's attendance at
constitutional convention, 152
Hutcheson, Francis, 117

Iconology (Richardson), *2,* 14
Independence, financial and intel-
lectual, 97
Ingres, Jean-Auguste-Dominique
Apotheosis of Napoleon, study for,
74, *77*
Jupiter and Thetis, 54, 55–56, 62,
65, 68
*Portrait of Napoleon I on His
Imperial Throne, 64,* 65, 68, 80,
220
*Inquiry Concerning the Principles of
Morals* (Hume), 198
Interior of Peale's Museum (Peale),
122, 122
Iphigénie (Gluck), 118
Irving, Washington, *Life of Wash-
ington,* 175

Jacob, 50
Jay, John, 4, 211
and Washington's attendance at
constitutional convention,
154–55
Jay's Treaty, 89, 186

Jefferson, Thomas, 24, 82, 107, 118,
132, 220, 221, 228
debt in later years, 96
and deposition-pietà scenes, 177
foreign policy, 91
and freedom for slaves, 96
on Genet, 94–95
on greatness of Washington and
Franklin, 198–99
on Hamilton's view of greatest
man, 137–38
and heroic age, 110–17
and heroic role models, 126
on Houdon, 128
on Houdon's statue of Washington, 221
on John Adams, 188–89
and Lafayette's imprisonment,
186
Notes on the State of Virginia, 233
portrayed in Franklin's laboratory, 200, *203*
and Society of the Cincinnati,
141, *145*
Sully portrait, 168, *169*
Tearoom at Monticello, 112, *113*
on Washington and Society of
the Cincinnati, 141
John Paul II, Pope, 165
Johnson, Lyndon B., 88
Johnson, Samuel, 51, 208
John Trumbull (Hughes), 143
Joshua, Washington compared to,
28–31
Journal of Congress, 172
Jupiter and Thetis (Ingres), *54,* 55–
56, 62, 65, 68

Kames, Henry Home, Lord, 100
Kennedy, John F., 109

)